Introduction to
The Philosophy of History

Introduction to
The Philosophy of History

G.W.F. HEGEL

with selections from
The Philosophy of Right

Translated, with Introduction,
by LEO RAUCH

Hackett Publishing Company
Indianapolis & Cambridge

G. W. F. Hegel: 1770–1831

Cover design by Listenberger Design & Associates
Interior design by Jared Carter

For further information, please address
Hackett Publishing Company, Inc.
P.O. Box 44937
Indianapolis, Indiana 46204

Library of Congress Cataloging in Publication Data
Hegel, Georg Wilhelm Friedrich, 1770-1831.
    [Vorlesungen über die Philosophie der Geschichte.
Einleitung. English]
    Introduction to The philosophy of history: with selections
from The philosophy of right / G.W.F. Hegel; translated, with
introduction, by Leo Rauch.
        p.   cm.
    Translation of: Vorlesungen über die Philosophie der
Geschichte. Einleitung. Also includes selections translated
from: Grundlinien der Philosophie des Rechts.
    Bibliography: p.
    ISBN 0-87220-057-4.   ISBN 0-87220-056-6 (pbk.)
    1. History—Philosophy.   I. Rauch, Leo.   II Title.
D16.8.H47413   1988
901—dc 19   88-29312
                                               CIP

Contents

Translator's Introduction

Georg Wilhelm Friedrich Hegel (1770–1831) lived in a time of startling changes. The American and French Revolutions, the Industrial Revolution, the Napoleonic Wars, the restructuring of European empires, and the rise of nationalism—all these, and more, inspired Hegel to look for a pattern, some order and meaning, in the diversity of historical events.

Born in Stuttgart in 1770, Hegel was a nineteen-year-old seminary student when the French Revolution sent its shock waves throughout Europe. Along with his two fellow students, Schelling and Hölderlin, Hegel was caught up in the heady enthusiasm of the revolutionary period. Autocracy was being swept away. But would the French people take hold of genuine freedom at last, and rule themselves as a free people? What ultimate rationality lay behind such apparently irrational events as the Terror? These were some of the problems which motivated Hegel's reflections on history.

After graduating from the seminary, Hegel briefly took a post as a family tutor, but in 1800 he joined his friend Schelling on the faculty of the University of Jena. At the time, this university was the philosophic center of Germany, and it was here that Hegel wrote his first major book, the brilliant *Phenomenology of Spirit*. In the *Phenomenology*, he sought to show how certain cultural outlooks or characteristic world views (e.g., those of medieval Christianity, the Enlightenment, the Terror) followed one another with logical necessity, so that each one led inevitably to the next. Tradition has it that he completed the book while hearing the gunfire from the battle of Jena, in October of 1806. When Napoleon captured the city, the university closed down and Hegel was out of a job.

For two years he edited a newspaper in another city, and then accepted the post of headmaster and lecturer in philosophy at a high school in Nuremberg. He continued to be a keen observer of contemporary politics, reading avidly the English and French newspapers, and writing articles on current issues. He did not hold another university post until 1816, when he was appointed professor of philosophy at the University of Heidelberg. He left there in 1818 to become professor of philosophy at the University of Berlin. By then he had published his formidable *Science of Logic* (1813; 1816), his *Encyclopedia of the Philosophical Sciences* (1817), and was soon to publish his *Philosophy of Right* (1821). At the time of the Berlin appointment Hegel was universally acknowledged to be one of the intellectual giants of his time, and his wide-ranging lectures on the philosophy of art, the philosophy of religion, the history of philosophy, and the philosophy of history won him an appreciative audience.

He died unexpectedly in a cholera epidemic in 1831, in the midst of an active and fruitful life devoted to the pursuit of reason. His contemporaries were stunned at the sudden loss, for it was felt that Hegel had many valuable contributions still to make to philosophy—perhaps expressing an all-embracing vision which would combine the central insights of the works he had published in his lifetime. To forward his program, a number of his friends and colleagues convened soon after his death to produce an edition of his collected works. They went beyond the works Hegel himself had published, gathering up his hand-written lecture notes and combining them with transcriptions of his lectures made by his student listeners. This resulted in his posthumous *Philosophy of Art*, the *Philosophy of Religion*, the *History of Philosophy*, and the *Philosophy of History*.

Even though Hegel had not prepared these materials for publication, these posthumous volumes amply reveal Hegel's characteristic keenness of insight, his penetrating awareness of life's paradoxical nature, and his deep sensitivity to the tortuous struggle of the human spirit in its concrete history. In the *Philosophy of History*, Hegel likens this struggle to the way an individual comes to maturity: in becoming self-conscious, one achieves full freedom, along with a responsibility to oneself. History, for Hegel, is the story of the development of the consciousness of freedom in the world—the development of the human spirit in time through the growth of *its own* self-consciousness.

In the *Philosophy of History* Hegel speaks of three "worlds"— actually three distinct world-outlooks: what Hegel calls the Oriental, the Greco-Roman, and the Germanic. These are linked only tenuously to specific times and geographical areas. But precisely because these "worlds" are not moored in a specific time or place, we may the more easily see them as standing in a *formal* relation to one another. In the Oriental World [taken in the broadest sense— e.g., ancient Egypt, China, etc.], only *one* person is free: the supreme monarch. In the Greco-Roman World, only *some* persons are free: those who are not slaves, women, aliens, et al. Finally in the Germanic World [i.e., the world of Christian Europe], *all* are free: by virtue of the spiritual identity accorded to all human individuals, all persons have the capacity for self-determination. In the relative degrees of freedom they permit, the three worlds stand in a dynamic relation to one another. History, for Hegel, is therefore a process of emancipation and enlightenment, with the aim of enabling us to construct a system of society wherein *everyone* can be regarded as free and autonomous, simply by virtue of being a person—conscious and rational.

This goal is not necessarily seen by history's participants. What Hegel calls the "Cunning of Reason" can make use even of irrational drives in history's players in order to achieve history's rational goal. The major actors on the stage of history, the "world-historical individuals" (e.g., Napoleon), are not in the least aware that the World-Spirit is using them for purposes of its own, not theirs. And when history has finished with them, it discards them.

Hegel's doctrines may be difficult to accept. Can we agree that the insane ambition that has so often moved the world-historical figures always leads to the fulfillment of rational goals, to the promoting of free and self-conscious social existence? Hegel was by no means blind to history's dark side, and indeed he spoke of history as a "slaughter-bench." Can we presume to say that some higher human goal is now nearer our grasp as a result of the universal suffering we have seen in our time?

If we adopt a wide enough perspective—say, we contrast ourselves with the earliest *Homo sapiens*—then we must surely see signs of progress. But it is the narrower range of comparison that poses the haunting questions. Thus what troubles us is whether the death and misery suffered by countless millions in this century can be seen to have contributed to some positive outcome. Even to ask that question seems a piece of monstrous arrogance, as though all that pain and death could be justified by any cause.

For Hegel, the goal of history can be said to be achieved when our individual and societal lives are fully in our control, so that we are able to give a conscious and rational shape to our lives as self-determining members of human society—a goal which an ancient Egyptian could hardly have imagined, let alone have hoped to achieve. It is this ideal that Hegel expresses in the Preface to his 1821 *Philosophy of Right*, with the phrase: "What is rational is real, and what is real is rational." *The rational is real*: Reason manifests itself in the world, and is "realized" in it in both senses of that word: reason is made real by fulfilling its own standard of rationality; and reason is grasped by reason itself—as in "I realize what I am saying"—in the self-consciousness that constitutes its freedom. *The real is rational*: The fulfilled reality is fully rational in the twofold sense of being fully transparent to reason, and also in being the product of rational forethought.

The highest fulfillment to human life on earth would be the harmonious synthesis of reason and society, so that the one principle shapes the other: "man is a rational animal" and "man is a social animal." The synthesis of these principles is an ideal as old as Plato. Hegel saw history as the struggle toward that end.

NOTE ON THE TEXT AND TRANSLATION

Hegel himself never published his *Philosophy of History,* but left only his lecture notes on the subject when he died. Afterward, these were combined with transcriptions that had been taken down by his student listeners. The 1840 compilation, prepared by Eduard Gans and Hegel's son Karl, is the version I have used (as reprinted in the 1928 Glockner edition of Hegel's *Sämtliche Werke*). The complete volume comprises over 500 pages, the greater portion being devoted to what we might call cultural history. In the 150-page Introduction, however, Hegel presents his *philosophy* of history, and that is the text of this translation.

Three other English translations known to me are those of Sibree (1857), Hartman (1953), and Nisbet (1975). I believe that I have avoided many of the weaknesses and corrected many of the errors in all three, and that the present work is clearer, more readable, and truer to Hegel.

In addition, this translation includes material not present in Hartman: Chapter Five, "The Geographical Basis of History" (interesting for what it says about America); and Chapter Six, "The Division of History." Finally, I have included as an Appendix paragraphs 341–360 of Hegel's *Philosophy of Right*. This is especially important because it is Hegel's own summary of the main themes of his philosophy of history. In his lectures, Hegel designates these paragraphs as the only substitute for a "textbook" he can offer to students of this subject. (See the footnote on the first page of Chapter One.) I have also supplied a bibliography of some Hegel texts and recent commentaries.

The division into chapters is my own doing. (Hartman's divisions are similar, although our headings differ.) In the German text, the first four chapters run undivided. The separation, however arbitrary, is justified by the increased readability.

It is by now traditional for Hegel's translators to refer to the difficulties of their task. I do so here only in order to shed light on Hegel as a thinker. In English, we like a word to have one and the same meaning throughout a given philosophic text. Hegel does not work that way. Some of his most salient words have entire clusters of meanings attached to them. Thus the problematic term *"Aufhebung"* means not only "negation" and "nullification" but also "elevation," "transcendence," and "retention"—among numerous other meanings. It would be bad enough if Hegel adopted a different meaning from one usage to the next, for we might then get the word's meaning from the context. Unfortunately, Hegel often has *all* of the various and even contradictory meanings in mind when he uses such a word. He works with positive as well as negative connotations, and he exploits their ambiguities. Indeed, it is the very essence of the Hegelian dialectic to show *how* a concept's meaning can be "negated" yet "retained" by being taken up to a higher order of meaning. That very negativity itself goes into the translation of a word such as *"Aufhebung."* The translator must choose one English word for each instance of the word's appearance, and the other meanings are retained in his mind but lost in the translated text. Some translators resort to an obscure word such as "sublation" to stand for the entire cluster of meanings in a technical way, but such a word lacks intuitive force. And to stay with that one word throughout only compounds the problem.

Another very troubling term is the notorious *"Geist"*—which means "spirit," but also "mind," "mentality," "soul," and "intellect." Most of the time, in the present text, Hegel uses *"Geist"* in its universal sense—as in "national spirit," rather than in the individual/subjective sense of "mind." (One could hardly speak of a "national mind.") Yet here, too, Hegel exploits the ambiguity: world history is a process of development which he likens to that of an individual's mind in growing up—and that metaphor could not work unless there were that ambiguity in the universal and individual senses of *"Geist."* Some translators of other works by Hegel have insisted on using the word "mind" throughout. I have almost always used "Spirit" in this translation, to show that I take the term in its universal/objective sense, rather than in the individual/subjective sense of "mind"; and by capitalizing it I try to suggest that I intend it in the special sense unique to Hegel.

Professor H.S. Harris made many remarks relating to my translation of other terms. Most often his comments pulled me in the direction of linguistic uniformity; at other times, his proposals argued for contextual elasticity. In a few of my translation-decisions I have quite deliberately departed from his thoughtful suggestions. For example, in regard to the terms *"allgemein," "besonder,"* and *"einzeln"* (respectively: "universal" *or* "general"; "particular"; and "individual" *or* "singular"), my choices were dictated by what I believed would best serve the aims of clarity as well as ease of understanding, but at the minimal sacrifice of exactitude. They would not necessarily have been my choices had I been at work on a text such as Hegel's *Science of Logic*.

ACKNOWLEDGMENT

My indebtedness to H.S. Harris of York University, in Toronto, goes far beyond what I have indicated in my remarks above, and deserves special acknowledgment. Professor Harris read the translation with his characteristically scrupulous care and insight. In almost every case, I was glad to follow his suggestions—backed as they always were by his matchless knowledge of Hegel's *oeuvre*. This volume is immeasurably better for his contribution to it.

Boston   Leo Rauch
Spring, 1988

Selected Bibliography

By Hegel

Philosophy of Right, trans. T. M. Knox. Oxford: Oxford University Press, 1967.
Philosophy of Mind, trans. W. Wallace and A.V. Miller. Oxford: Clarendon Press, 1971.
Phenomenology of Spirit, trans. A.V. Miller. Oxford: Clarendon Press, 1977.

On Hegel

Avineri, S., *Hegel's Theory of the Modern State*. Cambridge: Cambridge University Press, 1972.
Inwood, M., ed. *Hegel*. (Oxford Readings in Philosophy.) Oxford: Oxford University Press, 1985.
Kaufmann, W., ed. *Hegel's Political Philosophy*. New York: Atherton, 1970.
Löwith, K. *From Hegel to Nietzsche*. New York: Holt, Rinehart & Winston, 1964.
MacIntyre, A., ed. *Hegel: A Collection of Critical Essays*. New York: Doubleday Anchor, 1972.
Marcuse, H. *Reason and Revolution*. Boston: Beacon Press, 1960.
The Monist. Vol. 48, no. 1 (January, 1964). "Hegel Today" issue.
O'Brien, G.D. *Hegel on Reason and History*. Chicago: University of Chicago Press, 1975.
Rauch., L. *The Political Animal: Studies in Political Philosophy from Machiavelli to Marx*. Amherst: University of Massachusetts Press, 1981.

Ritter, J. *Hegel and the French Revolution*. Cambridge, Massachusetts: MIT Press, 1982.

Taylor, C. *Hegel and Modern Society*. Cambridge: Cambridge University Press, 1979.

Wilkins, B.T. *Hegel's Philosophy of History*. Ithaca: Cornell University Press, 1974.

Introduction to
The Philosophy of History

One
The Methods of History

The philosophic history of the world—this is the subject of these lectures. Thus we do not aim to draw from history any general reflections on it, nor to elucidate it with examples from its own content. Rather, our concern is with world history itself.* Before going any farther, we ought to clarify just what this is. To do so, we must go through the other methods of dealing with history. Altogether, there are three:

    I. Original history
    II. Reflective history
    III. Philosophic history

    I. FOR THE FIRST OF THESE, certain names will immediately conjure up a distinct picture of what I mean. Thus Herodotus, Thucydides, and other such historians primarily describe the actions, events, and situations they themselves have witnessed, and whose spirit they shared in. They translate what is externally present into the realm of mental representation, thereby bringing the outer into the inner—just as the poet works up the stuff of his own sensation into images for our minds. Of course, such original historians rely on the reports and accounts of others, since it is not possible for one person to have seen everything. But they use these sources as ingre-

---

* I can provide no textbook as a basis for this subject, but in my *Philosophy of Right*, paragraphs 341–360, I have presented the more precise concept of such a world history, along with the principles and periods that go into the consideration of it. [See Appendix, below.]

3

dients only, (just as the poet already possesses the civilized speech to which he owes so much). These historians bind together what is vanishing down the stream of time, and place it all in the Temple of Memory to give it immortality.

Legends, folksongs, traditions—these are to be excluded from original history, because they are obscure modes of memory, proper to the mentality of pre-literate peoples. On the contrary, in original history we are concerned with peoples who knew what they were and what they wanted. The foundation of observed and observable reality provides a firmer ground than the transient soil in which legends and epics have grown; these no longer make up the historic record of those peoples that have risen to a firm individuality.

These original historians, then, transform the events, actions, and situations present to them into works of representation. The content of these histories, therefore, cannot be of great external scope. Think of Herodotus in his *Persian Wars*, Thucydides in *The Peloponnesian War*, Guicciardini in his *History of Italy* (1536): their essential material is what is present and alive in their surrounding world. The culture of the author and of the events in his work, the spirit of the author and of the actions he tells of, are one and the same. He describes more or less what he has seen, or at least lived through. Short spans of time, the individual patterns of men and events—these are the singular, unreflected features out of which he composes his portrait of the time, in order to bring that picture to posterity with as much clarity as it had in his own direct observation or in the accounts of other direct witnesses. He is not concerned with offering reflections on these events, for he lives within the spirit of the times and cannot as yet transcend them. And if the author—like Caesar—belongs to the class of military leaders or statesmen, then it is *his* goals themselves that are the topic of his history.

We say that such a historian is not reflective, but that persons and nations themselves are directly present in his history. Yet against this there are the speeches, which we can read, for example, in Thucydides; these were surely not spoken as they are represented but were worked up by the writer of the history. Speeches, however, are actions among men, and indeed they are effective actions in their very essence. Of course, people often say that there were *mere* speeches and in so saying they want to show the innocuous nature of mere talk. But *that* talk is mere babble—and babble has the important advantage of being innocuous itself. But the speeches of nations to nations, or to nations and princes, are integral components of history. If such speeches —as, for example, those of Pericles, the most profoundly learned, the most genuine and noble statesman— are surely worked up by Thucydides, they are at least not alien to Pericles. In these speeches the speakers express the maxims held by their people, their own personality, their awareness of the political situation, as well as their moral and spiritual nature and their principles, aims and modes of action. What the original historian presents as their speech is not a borrowed consciousness but the speakers' own culture.

If one wishes to immerse oneself in the life of other nations, there are historians one must study deeply and devote time to. But there are not as many of them as one might think. They are the historians one might go to, not only for erudition but for deep and genuine enjoyment: we have already mentioned Herodotus, the Father (i.e., the originator) of history, as well as Thucydides; Xenophon's *The Persian Expedition* is an equally original book; Caesar's *Commentaries* are the simple masterwork of a great mind. In antiquity these historians necessarily were great captains and statesmen. In the Middle Ages, it was the bishops who were at the center of political activity, but it was the monks who wrote history (in the form of naive chronicles), and who were as isolated from events as the men of antiquity were involved in them.

In modern times all this has changed. Our culture is essentially intellectual, and it immediately converts all events into reports for intellectual representation. We have some excellent examples of this—simple and exact— especially war reports, which deserve to be set beside those of Caesar, and are even more instructive in their wealth of content and their account of methods and conditions. To these we may add the French *Memoires*, written by clever heads about small matters, and containing much in the way of anecdote lacking in historical foundation. Yet often there are true historical masterworks, such as the *Memoires* of Cardinal de Retz (written 1673–76), displaying a greater historical field. In Germany such masters are rare. Frederick the Great in his *Histoire de mon Temps* is a praiseworthy exception. These authors must actually be of high social standing. Only from a superior position can one truly see things for what they are and see everything, not when one has to peer upward from below, through a narrow opening.

II. THE SECOND METHOD OF WRITING HISTORY we can call the *reflective*. It is history whose presentation goes beyond the present in spirit, and does not refer to the historian's own time. Here, too, we can distinguish different types:

A. Universal history aims, in general, at an overview of the entire history of a people or a country, or of the world. Here the main thing is the elaboration of the historical material, which the historian approaches with *his* spirit—this being different from the spirit contained in the content. Especially important are the principles the author sets up for himself, based in part on the content and goals of the actions and events, and in part on the way he constructs the history. With us Germans, historical writing shows a great variety of reflection and intelligence—each historian taking it into his head to go his own peculiar way. The English and French generally know how history must be written, because they stand more securely on a basis of general and national culture. With us, each one concocts his own peculiar characteristic—and instead of writing history, we keep on looking for the way history ought to be written.

This first type of reflective history is linked directly to the foregoing mode—i.e., original history—if it has no other purpose than to present the entire history of a country. Compilations of this kind—including histories of Livy, Diodorus Siculus, and the *Swiss Histories* of Johannes von Müller (in 24 volumes, written from 1780 to 1808)—are highly commendable if done well. Certainly it is best if these historians approach the first mode and write so vividly that the reader can have the impression of hearing the events recounted by contemporaries and eye-witnesses. But the singular tone—which an individual must have who belongs to a specific culture—often is not adjusted to accord with the times which the history covers, and the spirit that speaks through the author is different from the spirit of the times for which he speaks.

Thus Livy lets the kings, consuls, and generals—of an older Rome—make speeches that are appropriate to a skilled lawyer of his own time, in glaring contrast to the received legends of antiquity, such as the crude fable of Menenius Agrippa. He also gives us descriptions of battles as though he had witnessed them. But the details of these battles might be used to describe the battles of any era; and the definiteness in their description contrasts with the lack of coherence and with the inconsistency dominant in other writings of his. The difference between a compiler like Livy and an original historian such as Polybius can best be seen if we compare the two, and note how Livy makes use of the historical material preserved in Polybius by extending and shortening that material. Similarly, Johannes von Müller, in striving to be true to the older times he describes, has given his history a hollow solemnity and a wooden, pedantic appearance. One would much rather read of the same matters in the *Swiss Chronicles* of old Tschudy (who lived 1505–72), where everything is more naive and natural, without the artificial and affected archaism.

A history of the kind that surveys long periods, or the entire history of the world, must in fact give up the individual presentation of particular reality, and make do with summaries and abridgements. It is abstract not only in the sense that events and actions have to be omitted, but in the further sense that Thought is the mightiest epitomist. A battle, a great victory, a siege—these are no longer what they were, but instead are drawn together into simple statements. When Livy tells of the wars with the Volsci, he occasionally says, shortly enough: "This year war was waged on the Volsci."

B. *A second type of reflective history* is the *pragmatic*. When we are occupied with a remote world of the past, that world becomes present to the mind through the mind's own activity—and that recaptured world is the mind's reward for its labor. The events vary, but they are connected into one pattern in their universal and inner meaning. This is what negates the event as past, and makes it present. Pragmatic reflections, abstract though they might be are thus what is in fact present, and they bring the accounts of the past to life in our present-day world. But whether reflections of this kind are really filled with interest and vitality depends on the mind of the author.

Here we must also mention, in particular, the moral reflections and moral instruction to be gained from history, when it is worked up for this purpose. While it is true that certain historical examples of goodness may be brought to bear for the moral education of children and the elevation of their minds in order to impress them with what is morally admirable, it is also true that the destinies of nations and states—with their interests, situations, and complexities—are a different field of knowledge. Rulers, statesmen, and nations are told that they ought to learn from the experience of history. Yet what experience and history teach us is this, that nations and governments have never learned anything from history, nor acted in accordance with the lessons to be derived from it. Each era has such particular circumstances, such individual situations, that decisions can only be made from within the era itself. In the press of world events, there is no help to be had from general principles, nor from the memory of similar conditions in former times—for a pale memory has no force against the vitality and freedom of the present. In this respect, nothing is more trite than the repeated appeal to Greek and Roman examples, which was so commonplace at the time of the French Revolution. No difference could be greater than that between the nature of those ancient peoples and our own time.*

Johannes von Müller had moral intentions of this sort in his universal history as well as in his Swiss history: he aimed to prepare moral "lessons" for the edification of princes, governments and nations, particularly for the Swiss (he made his own collection of lessons and reflections, and he often notes in his letters the exact number of reflections he has written out that week); but this cannot be counted as a part of the best things he produced. The only thing that can give truth and interest to reflections is the thoroughgoing, free, and comprehensive view of different situations and the deep sense of the fundamental idea—as, for example, in Montesquieu's *Spirit of the Laws* (1748). For this reason, *one* reflective history supersedes *another*. Each author has the materials available, so that each can consider himself equally capable of organizing them and working them up, thus validating his own spirit in them as the spirit of the time. Wearied of such reflective histories, we all too often

---

* See Hume's *Enquiry Concerning Human Understanding*, Section VIII, Part I: "Would you know the sentiments, inclinations, and course of life of the Greeks and Romans? Study well the temper and actions of the French and English. . . . Mankind are so much the same, in all times and places, that history informs us of nothing new or strange in this particular." [Translator's note.]

resort to the practice of describing an event from every vantage point. Such histories are in any case worth something, but for the most part they merely supply raw material. We Germans are satisfied with this; the French, on the contrary, ingeniously shape the past into a present and relate it to their present situation.

C. *The third type of reflective history* is the *critical*. It must be brought up here because it is the particular way in which history is treated in Germany at present. What is here presented is not history itself, but a history of historical writing, and a critical evaluation of historical accounts together with an inquiry into their truth and trustworthiness. What is meant to be exceptional, here, consists in the ingenuity of the author in extorting something new from the historical accounts, not in the things themselves. The French have contributed much that is profound and thoughtful in this field. All the same, they have not sought to validate this critical procedure as historical, but have rather organized their evaluations in the form of critical monographs.

Among us Germans, the so-called higher criticism has seized hold not only of philology in general but of historical literature. This higher criticism has supposedly justified the introduction of all the unhistorical abortions of an empty imagination. This is the other means of achieving "reality" in history: that is, by putting subjective notions in place of historical data. The bolder these notions are—i.e., the scantier the evidence on which they rest, and the more they contradict the most definite facts of history—the more excellent they are taken to be.

D. *The final type of reflective history* is that which directly presents itself as *specialized*, i.e., part of the greater whole. Although it does abstract from the whole, it does form a transition to philosophic world history, by taking universal viewpoints (e.g., the history of art, of law, or of religion). In our time, this type of conceptual history has been more developed and has been brought into prominence. Branches of this kind are related to the totality that is the history of a people—and the only question is whether the coherence of the totality has been made evident or has merely been sought in external circumstances. In the latter case, they appear as entirely accidental oddities of different peoples.

Accordingly, if reflective history has come to pursue general viewpoints, then we should notice where they are genuine. These viewpoints are not merely the outer thread, or an external order, but rather the inner guiding soul of the events and actions. For, like Mercury, the conductor of departed souls, the Idea is truly the guide of nations of the world. And Spirit, as its rational and necessary will, is what guides and has guided the course of events in the world. To recognize it—in the way it guides the world—is our present aim. And this leads to:

III. THE THIRD METHOD OF HISTORY, the *philosophic*. The two previous methods had no need of clarification, since their concept was self-explanatory. With the third method, however, there does seem to be a need for elucidation or justification.

The universal principle, however, is that the term "philosophy of history" signifies nothing other than the thoughtful consideration of history—[that is, the application of philosophic thought to history].

We cannot ever give up thinking; that is how we differ from the animals. There is a thinking in our perception, in our cognition and our intellect, in our drives and our volition (to the extent that these are human). But for that reason, the appeal to thinking may seem unsatisfying here, because in history our thinking is subordinated to the given and to what exists; it has all this as its basis and is governed by it. Philosophy, however, has thoughts of its own, brought forth by speculation from within itself and without reference to what is.

If the philosopher approaches history with thoughts of this kind, then he is dealing with history as a raw material, not to be left as it is, but to be construed according to thoughts, *a priori*.* But since history has merely to take in information—i.e., of what is and has been, of events and actions—and since it remains all the truer the more it confines itself to what is given, this approach seems to be in conflict with the proper concern of philosophy. And this contradiction, together with the reproach springing from it in regard to

---

* See Kant's essay, "The Idea of a Universal History from a Cosmopolitan Point of View" as an outstanding example of the *a priori* construal of history that Hegel means. [Translator's note.]

speculation, must here be clarified and resolved. But this is to be done without entering into the many corrections of the infinitely numerous and distorted views now held (or forever being reinvented) regarding the purpose, the interests and the handling of what is historical and its relation to philosophy.

TWO
Reason in History

The only thought which philosophy brings with it, in regard to history, is the simple thought of Reason—the thought that Reason rules the world, and that world history has therefore been rational in its course. This conviction and insight is a *presuppostion* in regard to history as such, although it is not a presupposition in philosophy itself.

In philosophy, speculative reflection has shown that Reason is the *substance* as well as the *infinite power*; that Reason is for itself the *infinite material* of all natural and spiritual life, as well as the *infinite form*, and that its actualization of itself is its content. (And we can stand by the term "Reason" here, without examining its relation and connection with "God" more closely.)

Thus Reason is the *substance* [of our historic world] in the sense that it is that whereby and wherein all reality has its being and subsistence. It is the *infinite power*, since Reason is not so powerless as to arrive at nothing more than the ideal, the ought, and to remain outside reality—who knows where—as something peculiar in the heads of a few people. Reason is the *infinite content*, the very stuff of all essence and truth, which it gives to its own *activity* to be worked up. For, unlike finite activity, it does not need such conditions as an external material, or given means from which to get its nourishment and the objects of its activity. It lives on itself, and it is itself the material upon which it works. Just as Reason is its own presupposition and absolute goal, so it is the activation of that goal in world history—bringing it forth from the inner source to external manifestation, not only in the natural universe but also in the spiritual. That this Idea is the True, the Eternal, simply the Power—that it reveals

12

itself in the world, and that nothing else is revealed in the world but that Idea itself, its glory and majesty—this, as we said, is what has been shown in philosophy, and it is here presupposed as already proven.

Those of you who are not yet acquainted with philosophy can at least be expected to come to these lectures on world history with the belief in Reason, with the desire, the thirst to know it. And indeed what must be presupposed as a subjective need in the study of the sciences is the desire for rational insight, for knowledge, not merely for a collection of facts. Thus, even if you do not bring to world history the thought and the knowledge of Reason, you ought at least to have the firm and unconquerable belief that there is Reason in history, together with the belief that the world of intelligence and self-conscious will is not subject to chance, but rather that it must demonstrate itself in the light of the self-conscious Idea.

But in fact I need not require this belief on your part in advance. What I have said so far, and will say again, is not just to be taken as a presupposition of our science, but as a summary of the totality—as the *result* of the discussion upon which we are embarking, a result that is known to *me* because I already know that totality. Thus it is the consideration of world history itself that must reveal its rational process—namely, that it has been the rational, necessary course of the World Spirit, the Spirit whose nature is indeed always one and the same, but which reveals this one nature in the world's reality. As I said, this must be the outcome of the study of history.

Yet we must take history as it is, and proceed historically, i.e., empirically. Among other things, we must not be misled by the professional historians, particularly the Germans, who possess great authority, and do precisely what they accuse philosophers of doing, namely creating *a priori* fabrications in history. For example, there is a widespread fabrication that there existed an original, primeval people, taught directly by God and having complete insight and wisdom, with a penetrating knowledge of all the laws of nature and spiritual truth; or that there were such or such priestly peoples; or, to speak of something more specific, that there was a Roman epic from which the Roman historians drew their earliest history, and so on. Let us leave all such *a priori* constructions to the clever professionals, for whom (in Germany) such constructions are not uncommon.

As the first condition to be observed, we could therefore declare that we must apprehend the historical faithfully. But with such general terms as "apprehend" and "faithfully" there lies an ambiguity. Even the ordinary, average historian, who believes and says that he is merely receptive to his data, is not passive in his thinking; he brings his categories along with him, and sees his data through them. In every treatise that is to be scientific, Reason must not slumber, and reflection must be actively applied. To him who looks at the world rationally, the world looks rational in return. The relation is mutual. But the various kinds of reflection, of possible viewpoints, of judgment even in regard to the mere importance and unimportance of facts (the most basic category in historical judgment)—all this does not concern us here.

In regard to the general conviction that Reason rules and has ruled in the world and likewise in world history, I would like to draw your attention to just two versions of that conviction. These will enable us to get closer to that main point which is so difficult, and at the same time to point ahead to our further discussion.

A. To begin with, there is the historical fact that the Greek, Anaxagoras, was the first to say that *nous*—understanding in general, or Reason—rules the world. By this he did not mean an intelligence as self-conscious reason, or a mind as such. We must take care to differentiate *nous* and "mind" from one another. The movement of the solar system follows immutable laws. These laws are its Reason. But neither the sun, nor the planets that revolve around it according to these laws, have any consciousness of them.

Such a thought—that there is Reason in nature, that nature is governed unchangeably by general laws—does not surprise us. We are accustomed to thinking in this way, and we do not make much of it. I have merely mentioned this historical fact to make you aware of what history shows: namely, that a thought which seems trivial to us was not always commonplace in the world, but rather was epoch-making in the history of the human spirit. Aristotle says of Anaxagoras, as the originator of this thought, that he appeared like a sober man among the drunken ones. From Anaxagoras, Socrates took it up, and it immediately became the dominant thought in philosophy (except for the philosophy of Epicurus, which ascribed all events to chance).

Plato has Socrates say: "I was delighted with this thought, and I was hoping to have found a teacher who would explain nature according to Reason, and show in each particular thing its particular purpose, as well as the universal purpose in the totality. Not for a great fortune would I have given up this hope. But how disappointed I was when I so eagerly took up the writings of Anaxagoras himself, and I found that he brought in to his explanation merely external causes such as Air, the Ether, Water and the like—instead of Reason." [*Phaedo*, 97c-98c]

We can see that what Socrates found so unsatisfying in the principle of Anaxagoras was not the principle itself, but rather Anaxagoras' failure to apply it to concrete nature: that this nature was not understood or conceived on the basis of that principle, but that that principle was held to as something abstract. Nature was not grasped as a development of Reason, not as an organic whole brought forth by Reason. At the very outset, therefore, I want to call your attention to the difference between maintaining a conception, a principle, a truth in a merely abstract way, and carrying it through to a fuller determination and a concrete development. This difference—i.e., between the abstract and the concrete—is basic to all philosophy as well. Thus at the end of our discussion of world history, we shall be returning to this point especially, in dealing with the most recent political situation.

B. The second version of the thought that Reason rules the world is related to a further application of it, with which we are well acquainted in the form of the religious truth that the world is not subject to chance and to external contingencies, but that it is ruled by a *Providence*. I explained earlier that I do not wish to make any demands on your belief in this principle of Providence. Yet I might appeal to your belief in it in this *religious form*—if, that is, the distinctive character of the science of philosophy allowed presuppositions to count at all. To put it in another way, the appeal to your belief is not necessary because the science we wish to discuss will itself provide the proof of the correctness of that principle, if not the proof of its truth. The truth, then, that there is a divine providence presiding over the events of the world, corresponds to the stated principle: for divine providence is wisdom with infinite power, realizing its own ends, i.e., the absolute, rational end-goal of the world, while Reason is Thought, quite freely determining itself.

But now we also see a difference emerging. There is, indeed, a contradiction between this belief in providence and our principle—rather like the difference between the dictum of Anaxagoras and the expectations of Socrates in regard to it. That belief in a providence is indefinite in the same way: it does not advance to any definite conclusion, as applied to the totality of things and to the all-encompassing course of world history. To explain history, however, means to reveal the passions of human beings, their talents, their active powers. This definiteness of providence is what is usually taken for its *plan*. Yet it is this very plan that is supposed to be hidden from our view, so that we would be presumptuous to want to understand it.

The ignorance of Anaxagoras, as to how Reason manifests itself in reality, was sincere. The awareness of that thought—whether in him or in Greece in general—had not yet gone any further. He could not yet apply his principle to the concrete events, and understand concrete reality in terms of that principle. It was Socrates who took the first step towards grasping the union of the concrete with the universal. Anaxagoras, therefore, was not explicitly opposed to such an application of the universal to the concrete. But the belief in providence *is* opposed at least to the large-scale application of the principle, and to our comprehending the plan of providence. Here and there, in particular cases, the application is allowed: pious souls see in certain individual events not merely the workings of chance, but of God's hand—for example, when an individual in great distress and need receives help unexpectedly. But these purposes themselves are of a restricted sort, for they are only the particular purposes of this individual.

In world history, however, we are concerned with "individuals" that are nations, with wholes that are states. Accordingly, we cannot stop at the (so to speak) "retail" version of the belief in providence—still less can we be content with the merely abstract, indefinite belief which goes only so far as the general view that there is a providence, and says nothing of its more definite acts. On the contrary, we must seriously try to recognize the ways of providence, and to connect its means and manifestations in history—relating these to that universal principle.

But in mentioning the possibility of our knowing the plan of divine providence in general, I have touched on a question that has become prominent in our own time: the question about the possibility of our knowing God—or, inasmuch as it has ceased to be a question, there is the doctrine (which has now become a prejudice) that it is impossible to know God. Holy Scripture commands it as our highest duty not only to love God but also to know God. But in direct opposition to this, there now prevails the denial of what is there written: that it is the Spirit that leads us to truth, that the Spirit knows all things and penetrates even to the depths of the Godhead. *

When the Divine Being is placed beyond the reach of our knowing and beyond human affairs altogether, we gain the convenience of indulging in our own imaginings. We are thereby excused from having to give our knowledge some relation to the Divine and the True. On the contrary, the vanity of human knowledge and subjective feeling receives a complete justification for itself. And when pious humility places the knowing of God at a distance, it knows full well what it has thereby gained for its arbitrariness and vain efforts.

I could not avoid mentioning the connection between our thesis (that Reason rules the world and has ruled it) and the question about the possibility of our knowing God, since I did not want to dodge the accusation that philosophy shuns (or must shun) all discussion of religious truths due to a bad conscience about them. On the contrary, in modern times we have come to the point where philosophy has to take up the defense of religious truths against many types of theological doctrine. In the Christian religion God has revealed Himself: that is to say, He has allowed human beings to understand what He is, so that He is no longer hidden and secret. With this possibility of our knowing God, the obligation to know Him is placed upon us. God wants no narrow-minded souls and empty heads for His children. Rather, He wants those who (however poor in spirit) are rich in the knowledge of Him, and who place the highest value in this knowledge of Him. The development

---

* See I Corinthians 2:10. "God has revealed these things to us through the Spirit. For the Spirit searches all things, even the depths of God." [Translator's note.]

of the thinking spirit, which began from this basis in the revelation of the Divine Being, must finally come to the point where what was originally present only to feeling and to the imagining spirit, can now be grasped by thought. And the time must finally come when we comprehend the rich product of creative Reason that is world history.

For some time, it was customary to admire God's wisdom at work in animals, in plants, and in the destinies of individuals. If we grant that providence reveals itself in such objects and materials, then why not also in world history? Here, the material seems too great. Yet the divine wisdom, i.e., Reason, is one and the same on the large scale and on the small, and we must not consider God to be too weak to apply His wisdom on a large scale. In our knowledge, we aim for the insight that whatever was intended by the Eternal Wisdom has come to fulfillment—as in the realm of nature, so in the realm of spirit that is active and actual in the world. To that extent our approach is a theodicy, a justification of the ways of God. Leibniz attempted a theodicy in metaphysical terms, using indefinite abstract categories—so that when once the evil in the world was comprehended in this way, the thinking mind was supposed to be reconciled to it. Nowhere, in fact, is there a greater challenge to such intellectual reconciliation than in world history. This reconciliation can be achieved only through the recognition of that positive aspect, in which the negative disappears as something subordinate and overcome. It is attained (on the one hand) through the awareness of the true end-goal of the world, and (on the other) through the awareness that this end has been actualized in the world and that the evil has not prevailed in it in any ultimate sense.

For this purpose, however, the mere belief in *nous* and providence is still quite inadequate. "Reason"—which is said to rule the world—is just as indefinite a term as "Providence." We hear Reason spoken of, without anyone being able to say just what its definition is, or its content (according to which we could judge whether something is rational or irrational). To grasp Reason in its definition—that is of primary importance. If we merely stick to the bare term, "Reason", throughout, the rest of what we say is just words. With these declarations behind us, we can go on to the second viewpoint we wish to consider in this Introduction.

Three
Freedom, the Individual, and the State

If we think of Reason in its relation to the world, then the question of the *definition* of Reason in itself coincides with the question about the *final goal* of the world. Implicit in that latter term is the suggestion that the goal is to be realized, made actual. There are two things to be considered here: the content of that goal (i.e., the definition itself, as such), and its actualization.

At the outset we must note that our object—*world history*—takes place in the realm of Spirit. The term "world" includes both physical and mental nature. Physical nature impinges on world history as well, and from the very beginning we shall have to draw attention to the fundamental relations [between the two natures] in the definition. But it is Spirit, and the process of its development, that is the substance of history. Nature in itself, which is likewise a rational system in its particular and characteristic element, is not our concern here, except as related to Spirit.

Spirit is to be observed in the theater of world history, where it has its most concrete reality. In spite of this, however (or rather in order for us to grasp the universal aspect in this mode of Spirit's concrete reality), we must set forth, before all else, some abstract definitions of the *nature of Spirit*. These can, of course, be no more than mere assertions here. This is not the place to go into the Idea of Spirit in a speculative fashion, for what can be said in an introduction is simply to be taken historically—as a presupposition which (as we said) has either been worked out and proven elsewhere, or else is to receive its verification only as the outcome of the science of history itself.

19

We have therefore to address the following topics:

    I. The abstract characteristics of the nature of Spirit
   II. The means Spirit uses in order to realize its Idea
  III. The shape taken on by Spirit in its complete realization in the world—the State.

    I. THE NATURE OF SPIRIT. This can be seen by looking at its complete antithesis—matter. Just as the essence of matter is gravity [that is, in being determined by a force outside it], so the essence of Spirit is its freedom [that is, in its self-determination]. Everyone will immediately agree that Spirit is endowed with freedom, among other characteristics. Philosophy, however, teaches us that all the characteristics of Spirit subsist only by means of freedom; that all of them are only the means to freedom, and that they seek and produce only freedom. This is one of the truths of speculative philosophy: that freedom is the only truth of Spirit.

    Matter has weight insofar as it strives toward a central point outside itself. It is essentially composed of parts which are separable. It seeks its unity, which would be its own negation, its opposite. If it were to achieve this, it would no longer be matter but would have perished. It strives toward the ideal, for in unity [i.e., in being self-determining, self-moving], matter is idealized.

    Spirit, on the other hand, is that which has its center in itself. Its unity is not outside itself; rather, it has found it within its own self. It is in its own self and alone unto itself. While matter has its "substance" [i.e., its source of support] outside itself, Spirit is autonomous and self-sufficient, a Being-by-itself (*Bei-sich-selbst-sein*). But this, precisely, is freedom—for when I am dependent, I relate myself to something else, something which I am not; as dependent, I cannot be without something which is external. I am free when I exist independently, all by myself. This self-sufficient being is self-consciousness, the consciousness of self.

    Two things must be distinguished in consciousness: first, the fact *that* I know; and second, *what* I know. In self-consciousness, the two—subject and object—coincide. Spirit knows itself: it is the judging of its own nature, and at the same time it is the activity of coming to itself, of producing itself, making itself actually what it is in itself potentially.

According to this abstract definition, we can say of world history that it is the exhibition of the Spirit, the working out of the explicit knowledge of what it is potentially. Just as the germ of the plant carries within itself the entire nature of the tree, even the taste and shape of its fruit, so the first traces of Spirit virtually contain all history.

In the world of the ancient Orient, people do not yet know that the Spirit—the human as such—is free. Because they do not know this, they are not free. They know only that *one* person is free; but for this very reason such freedom is mere arbitrariness, savagery, stupified passion; or even a softness or tameness of passion, which is itself a mere accident of nature and therefore quite arbitrary. This *one* person is therefore only a despot, not a free man.

It was among the Greeks that the consciousness of freedom first arose, and thanks to that consciousness they were free. But they, and the Romans as well, knew only that *some* persons are free, not the human as such. Even Plato and Aristotle did not know this. Not only did the Greeks have slaves, therefore—and Greek life and their splendid freedom were bound up with this—but their freedom itself was partly a matter of mere chance, a transient and limited flowering, and partly a hard servitude of the human and the humane.

It was first the Germanic peoples, through Christianity, who came to the awareness that *every* human is free by virtue of being human, and that the freedom of spirit comprises our most human nature. This awareness arose first in religion, in the innermost region of Spirit. But to introduce this principle into worldly reality as well: that was a further task, requiring long effort and civilization to bring it into being. For example, slavery did not end immediately with the acceptance of the Christian religion; freedom did not suddenly prevail in Christian states; nor were governments and constitutions organized on a rational basis, or indeed upon the principle of freedom.

This application of the principle of freedom to worldly reality—the dissemination of this principle so that it permeates the worldly situation—this is the long process that makes up history itself. I have already drawn attention to the distinction between a principle as such and its application, its introduction and implementation in the actuality of spirit and life. This distinction is fundamental to our science, and it must be kept in mind. Just as this distinction was noted in a preliminary way with regard to the Christian principle of self-consciousness and freedom, so it has its essential place in regard to the principle of freedom in general. World history is the progress in the consciousness of freedom—a progress that we must come to know in its necessity.

Above, I made a general statement regarding the different levels in the awareness of freedom—namely, that the Orientals knew only that *one* person is free; the Greeks and Romans that *some* are free; while *we* know that *all* humans are implicitly free, *qua* human. At the same time, this statement gives us the division of world history and the basis for our consideration of it. But this is noted merely provisionally and in passing. We must first explain some other concepts.

The *final goal of the world*, we said, is Spirit's consciousness of its freedom, and hence also the actualization of that very freedom. This, then, is what characterizes the spiritual world—and this therefore is the substantially real world, to which the physical world is subordinate (or, to say this in speculative terms, the physical world has no truth as against the spiritual). But this "freedom," as so far described, is itself indefinite and infinitely ambiguous. As the highest of concepts it carries with it infinitely many misunderstandings, confusions and errors, and comprises all possible excesses within it. Never has all this been better known and felt than at the present time. For the time being, however, we must content ourselves with using it in that general sense.

We have also drawn attention to the importance of the infinite difference between the principle, which is as yet merely implicit, and that which is real. But at the same time it is freedom in itself that contains the infinite necessity of bringing itself to consciousness (for in its very concept it is knowledge of itself) and thereby to reality. Freedom is for itself the goal to be achieved, and the only goal of Spirit.

It is this final goal—freedom—toward which all the world's history has been working. It is this goal to which all the sacrifices have been brought upon the broad altar of the earth in the long flow of time. This is the one and only goal that accomplishes itself and fulfills itself—the only constant in the change of events and conditions, and the truly effective thing in them all. It is this goal that is God's will for the world. But God is the absolutely perfect Being, and He can therefore will nothing but Himself, His own will. The nature of His will, however—i.e., His own nature, that is what we are here calling the Idea of freedom (since we are translating the religious image into philosophic thought). The question that now follows immediately, then, can be this: What means does this Idea of freedom use for its realization? This is the second point to be considered.

II. THE MEANS OF SPIRIT. This question—as to the *means* whereby freedom develops itself into a world—leads us into the phenomenon of history itself. While freedom as such is primarily an internal concept, its means are external: namely, the phenomena which present themselves directly before our eyes in history. Our first look at history convinces us that the actions of human beings stem from their needs, their passions, their interests, their characters and talents. And it appears that the only springs of action in this theater of activity, and the mainsprings, are these needs, passions, and interests. Of course, the play also involves universal aims, benevolence, noble patriotism, and so on. But these virtues and their universality are insignificant in their relation to the world and its doings.

We might well see the ideal of Reason realized in these subjective individuals themselves and in their sphere of influence, but individuals are of slight importance compared to the mass of the human race; likewise, the scope of their virtues is relatively restricted in its range. Instead, it is the passions, the aims of particular interests, the satisfaction of selfish desire that are the most forceful things. They get their power from the fact that they observe none of the limits which the law and morality would seek to impose upon them—and from the fact that these forces of nature are closer and more immediate to human beings than the artificial and tedious discipline toward order and moderation, toward law and morality.

When we look at this drama of human passions, and observe the consequences of their violence and of the unreason that is linked not only to them but also (and especially) to good intentions and rightful aims; when we see arising from them all the evil, the wickedness, the decline of the most flourishing nations mankind has produced, we can only be filled with grief for all that has come to nothing. And since this decline and fall is not merely the work of nature but of the will of men, we might well end with moral outrage over such a drama, and with a revolt of our good spirit (if there is a spirit of goodness in us). Without rhetorical exaggeration, we could paint the most fearful picture of the misfortunes suffered by the noblest of nations and states as well as by private virtues—and with that picture we could arouse feelings of the deepest and most helpless sadness, not to be outweighed by any consoling outcome. We can strengthen ourselves against this, or escape it, only by thinking that, well, so it was at one time; it is fate; there is nothing to be done about it now. And finally—in order to cast off the tediousness that this reflection of sadness could produce in us and to return to involvement in our own life, to the present of our own aims and interests—we return to the selfishness of standing on a quiet shore where we can be secure in enjoying the distant sight of confusion and wreckage.

But as we contemplate history as this slaughter-bench, upon which the happiness of nations, the wisdom of states, and the virtues of individuals were sacrificed, the question necessarily comes to mind: What was the ultimate goal for which these monstrous sacrifices were made? And from this there usually follows the question which we made the starting-point of our consideration. And in this perspective the events that present such a grim picture for our troubled feeling and thoughtful reflection have to be seen as the *means* for what we claim is the substantial definition, the absolute end-goal or, equally, the true *result* of world history.

From the outset we have altogether avoided taking the path that goes from that picture of the particular events to the universal meaning. In any case, it is no service to those emotional reflections to rise above those feelings and in that way to solve the riddles of providence which the mournful view has given up on. It is far more characteristic of such reflections to enjoy the misery of the empty and fruitless sublimities of that negative outcome. We must return, therefore, to our original standpoint; and the elements that we wish to adduce will also contain the essential determinations through which the questions arising from that picture of human suffering can be answered.

The *first* thing we note is what we have already remarked upon, but which cannot be repeated too often, since it concerns the matter at hand: namely, that what we have called the principle, the final goal, the determination, or the nature and concept of Spirit, is only something general and abstract. A principle, or rule, or law is something internal which, whatever truth it has within it, is not completely actual. Aims, principles, and the like are, to begin with, in our thoughts—only in our inner intentions but not yet to be found in reality. What is implicit in itself is a possibility, a potentiality, but it has not yet emerged from its own inwardness into outer existence.

For actuality, there must be a *second* element added—and that is activity or actualization. The principle of this is the will, i.e., human activity in general. Only through this activity is the concept (along with its implicit determinations) realized, actualized—for these aims and principles are not immediately valid in and of themselves. The activity which puts them into operation and into existence is that which stems from human need, drive, inclination, and passion. I bring something into act and being because it suits me to do so: I must be involved in it; in acting on my desires I must be satisfied. A purpose for which I am to be active must in some way be my purpose as well. My own purpose must in some way be satisfied in it, even if the purpose for which I am active also has many other aspects that do not concern me. This is the infinite right of the subjective individual, to satisfy himself in his activity and work. If people are expected to have an interest in something, they themselves must be involved in it, and they must find their own sense of self satisfied in it.

There is a misunderstanding to be avoided here. It may be said of an individual, reproachfully, that he is an "interested party"—namely, that he is out for his private advantage, without regard for the common interest; he cloaks his own advantage in it, and even sacrifices the common interest in favor of his own. Yet one who is active in behalf of something is not merely "interested" but is interested *in it*. Language expresses this difference correctly. Nothing happens therefore, nothing is accomplished, unless the individuals involved are satisfied as well. They are particular persons, and this means that they have their own particular needs, drives, and interests. Among these needs there is not only one's own need and will, but also one's individual insight, conviction, or at least one's own viewpoint (if the need for argument, for understanding, and for reasoning is at all aroused). Hence people demand, as well, that if they are expected to be active in behalf of something, then it should be in accord with their views—so that their opinions can be in sympathy with it, whether in regard to the utility of it, or their own rights or advantage. This is especially an essential aspect of our time, in which people are less drawn to something by their trust in authority, and would prefer to devote their activity to a cause on the basis of their own understanding of it, their independent conviction and opinions.

We say, therefore, that nothing at all has come to pass without the interest of those whose activity is involved in it. And since we call an interest a "passion"—when all of one's individuality, to the neglect of all other interests and purposes one might have, is placed in the service of some cause; and every fiber of one's being, every last ounce of will-power is committed to it, so that all of one's needs and forces are concentrated upon it—we must assert as a general proposition that *nothing great* has been accomplished in the world *without passion*.

There are two elements that enter into our topic: the first is the Idea, the other is human passion; the first is the warp, the other the woof in the great tapestry of world history that is spread out before us. The concrete meeting point and union of the two is in ethical freedom in the state. We have already spoken of the Idea of freedom, as the essential nature of Spirit and the final goal of history. Passion is often seen as something that is not quite right, something more or less evil: the human being ought to have no passions; and the term "passion" is not quite the right word for what I want to express. What I generally understand by this word is human activity stemming from individual interests, from special goals or from self-seeking purposes if you like; but "passion" occurs when people place the entire energy of their will and character in these goals, sacrificing something else that might well be a goal, or even everything else.

This particular "passionate" content is so bound up with a person's will, that it is inseparable from it and comprises all that determines it; through it, the person is what he is. What is *there* is the individual, not Man in general. It is not Man that exists, but the specific individual. The term "character" expresses this uniqueness of will and intelligence as well; but "character" embraces all the particularities of the person, the modes of behavior in private relationships, etc., and this very uniqueness is asserted in nothing other than a person's effectiveness and activity.

I shall therefore use the term "passion" to signify the particular uniqueness of a person's character—to the extent that the uniqueness of will does not have a merely private content, but is also what drives and motivates actions of a universal scope. "Passion" is primarily the subjective and thus the formal aspect of energy, of will and activity, so that the content or goal remains as yet undetermined. At the same time it is there in one's own conviction, one's own insight and conscience. What matters is always the content of my conviction, the aim of my passion, and whether the one or the other is more genuine. But conversely, whichever is more genuine will enter into existence and become actual.

From this comment about the second essential element in the realization of a historical aim, it follows (if, for a moment, we look at the state) that a state is well constituted and internally strong if the private interest of the citizens is united with the universal goal of the state, so that each finds its fulfillment and realization in the other. This is a proposition of the highest intrinsic importance. But before this unity is brought into being, the state must undergo much struggle with private interests and passions, in a long and hard discipline of them. And the state needs many institutions, devices and practical arrangements, together with long struggles of the understanding, before it arrives at an awareness of what is appropriate to its goal. The era of such a unity constitutes the period of a state's flowering, the time of its excellence, power, and prosperity.

But world history does not begin with any conscious goal, such as we find in the particular spheres of human life. The simple social instinct of human beings already involves the conscious goal of securing life and property; and insofar as this life in common has already come into being, that goal is extended further. World history begins with its universal goal: the fulfillment of the concept of Spirit—still only *implicit* (*an sich*), i.e., as its nature. That goal is the inner, indeed the innermost, unconscious drive; and the entire business of world history is (as we said) the work of bringing it to consciousness.

Thus, what we called the subjective aspect—needs, drives, passions, particular interests, as well as opinions and subjective views—all this is immediately apparent to consciousness (*für sich*). It makes its entrance in the guise of a natural being, or of natural will. This imponderable mass of wills, interests, and activities—these are the tools and means of the World Spirit for achieving its goal, to elevate it to consciousness and to actualize it. And this goal is none other than to find itself, to come to itself, and to behold itself as actuality. But since those very life-forms of individuals and nations, in seeking to satisfy their own interests, are at the same time the tools and means of something higher and greater (of which they know nothing and which they fulfill unconsciously), all this could well be questioned, and it has been questioned. It has been denied, decried, and scorned in many ways as mere dreaming, mere "philosophy."

But on this question I have made my position clear from the very beginning. I laid down our presupposition (which is to appear only at the end, as the result of our investigation) and our belief, that Reason rules the world, which means that it has ruled history as well. Everything else is subordinate in relation to this universal and substantial Reason, in and for itself; it serves that Reason as its means. Moreover, this Reason is immanent in historical existence, and fulfills itself in and through it. The union of the universal, existing in and for itself, with the individual subjective aspect, so that this union alone is the truth—all this is speculative, and it is handled in this general form in metaphysical logic. But in the course of the world history itself, conceived as being still on the march, the pure end-goal of history is still not the content of need and interest; and although need and interest are unaware of the end-goal, the universal is still implicit in particular goals and fulfills itself in them.

The question [as to the union of the universal and the subjective] also takes the form of the union of *freedom* and *necessity*. For we regard the immanent development of Spirit as necessary because it is in and for itself, while we ascribe to freedom whatever appears in the conscious will of human beings as their interest. Since the speculative metaphysical aspect of this connection belongs to the sphere of logic, we cannot analyze it here. We can only mention the main points relevant to it.

It is demonstrated in philosophy that the Idea proceeds to its infinite antithesis: on the one hand there is the Idea in its freely universal mode wherein it remains self-sufficient (*bei sich*); and on the other hand there is the Idea as pure abstract reflection into itself (*in sich*), which is formal being for itself (*für sich*)—the ego or the formal freedom which belongs only to Spirit. Thus, on the one side, the universal Idea subsists as the substantial totality of things; and on the other side as the abstractness of arbitrary free will. This reflection into itself is the individual self-consciousness; it is the Other to the Idea in general, and thus it subsists in absolute finitude. For this very reason this Other is the finitude, the determinate element for the universal absolute: it is the side of the Absolute's existence, the ground of its formal reality, and the ground for the reverence due to God.

To grasp the absolute bonding of this antithesis—that is the profound task of metaphysics. Moreover, with the general positing of this finitude, all particularity is posited. In a formal sense, the Will wills itself, asserting the [singular] ego in everything that it intends and does. Even the pious individual wants to be saved, to be blessed [thus asserting his selfhood]. This pole of the antithesis, the individual existing for himself, is a particular entity—in contrast to the absolute universal essence—and it is as such that he knows this particularity of his and wills it. He is altogether at the standpoint of appearance. This is the sphere of particular aims, where the individuals assert themselves in their particularity, fulfilling it and actualizing it.

This standpoint, then, is also the standpoint of happiness or unhappiness. That individual is happy who has accommodated his existence to his particular character, will, and arbitrariness, so that he enjoys himself in his existence. But world history is not the place for happiness. Periods of happiness are empty pages in history, for they are the periods of harmony, times when the antithesis is missing. As reflection into self, this freedom is altogether abstract, it is the formal element of the activity of the absolute Idea. Activity is the unifying middle term of the syllogism: one pole is the universal, the Idea that rests in the inner pit of Spirit; the other pole is externality as such, objective matter. Activity is the middle term which translates the universal and internal into external objectivity.

I will try to make what I have said more evident and clear by giving some examples.

Building a house is, to begin with, an inner goal and purpose. As the means to that end, there are particular materials—iron, wood, stone. The elements are applied, in order to work up these materials: fire to melt the iron; air to blow up the fire; water to turn the wheels for cutting the wood, etc. The result is that the air, which helped in building the house, is now shut out by the house, since it excludes the wind; similarly the house keeps out streams of water because it excludes the rain; and insofar as the house is made fireproof it excludes the destructiveness of fire. The stones and beams are obedient to earth's gravity, and because they press downward high walls are set up. Thus the elements are utilized according to their nature, and yet they cooperate toward a product by which they themselves are being limited. In a similar way the human passions satisfy themselves; they fulfill their goals according to their natural determination and they bring forth the edifice of human society, in which they have provided for law and order as forces *against* themselves (i.e., restraining those passions).

The above-mentioned connection further entails the following: namely, that in world history the outcome of human actions is something other than what the agents aim at and actually achieve, something other than what they immediately know and will. They fulfill their own interests, but something further is thereby brought into being, something which is inwardly involved in what they do but which was not in their consciousness or part of their intention.

As an analogous example, let us consider the case of a man who, for revenge (and perhaps "justly," i.e., in return for an unjust injury) sets fire to another man's house. The immediate act is thus linked to further effects [on neighboring properties], i.e., effects which are in themselves external to the act and do not intrinsically belong to it. As such, the act involves merely the holding of a small flame to a small part of a roof beam. As yet, nothing more than this has been done—but further effects will follow of themselves. The ignited portion of the beam is connected to its other parts, and these to the woodwork of the entire house, this house to other houses nearby—and so a widespread conflagration ensues, which affects many more people than the one against whom the act of vengeance was directed, consuming their goods and property, and even costing many of them their lives. This result lay neither in the act as such, nor in the intention of the man who started it all.

But the action has yet another general aspect: the aim of the man who perpetrated the act of arson was to be revenged upon one individual through the destruction of his property; but arson is also a crime, and entails a punishment. This may not have been in the consciousness of the perpetrator, still less in his intention. But this is [entailed in] his act in itself—and these are the universal, substantial aspects of it that are brought about by it. It is precisely this that should be kept in mind in this example: that there can be something more involved in the immediate action than what is in the intention or the consciousness of the agent. The example has a further implication, however: the substance of an action, and thus the action itself, can turn against the agent, recoiling against him, to destroy him.

This union of the two poles—the realization of the universal Idea in immediate actuality, and the elevation of the singular [agency] into universal truth—occurs, first of all, under the presupposition of the distinctness of the two sides and their indifference toward one another. In their actions, the agents have finite aims and particular interests, but they also know and think. The content of their aims is permeated by the universal and essential determinations of what is right, good, duty, etc. (Bare desire, volition in its crude and savage form, falls outside the theater and sphere of world history.) And these universal determinations, which are also the guidelines for aims and actions, have a specific content; for something as empty of content as the Good or the Good Will has no place at all in living actuality. If men are to act, they must not only will the good, but they must also know whether this or that is good.

But as for the question of just what is good or not good, right or not right—in the ordinary situations of private life, that question is answered by the laws and customs of a state. There is no great difficulty in knowing what these are. Every individual has his station in life, and he knows, on the whole, what the right and honorable course of action is. To declare, in ordinary private relations, that it is so difficult to choose what is right and good; to see a superior morality in finding difficulties and raising scruples—all this rather indicates an evil and perverse will. This is a will that seeks to evade its duties, which are not hard to know; or at best we may ascribe this to an idleness of thought, a small-minded will that gives itself not much to do, and thus falls into self-indulgence and moral smugness.

The situation is quite different in regard to the great historical relations. It is here that we find the great collisions between, on one hand, the system of established and recognized duties, laws and rights, and, on the other, the possibilities which stand opposed to that system. These are possibilities that are injurious to the established order, destroying its foundations and its very existence—yet they have a content that can appear to be good, advantageous on the whole, even essential and necessary. These possibilities now become historical. They involve a universal concept, but one of a different sort from that which serves as the basis for the continued existence of a people or a state. This universal concept is a moving force of the productive Idea, an element of the truth that is forever striving toward itself, pressing on toward itself. The historical men—the *world-historical individuals*—are those whose aims embody a universal concept of this kind.

Caesar was such a man. At one point he was in danger of losing the position to which he had raised himself—a position, if not of predominance, at least of equality with the others who stood at the head of the state. Indeed, he was in danger of falling into the power of those who were about to become his enemies. These enemies, though they were pursuing their personal aims, had the formal state-structure on their side, with all the might of apparent legality. Caesar fought to retain his position, honor, and security—and since his opponents held power over the provinces, Caesar's victory over these men amounted to the conquest of the entire Roman empire. Thus, although he left the form of the state-structure unchanged, Caesar became the sole ruler of the state. The accomplishing of his originally negative aim—i.e., the autocratic control of Rome—was at the same time an essential determination in the history of Rome and of the world. It was not only the achievement of his personal victory; it was also an instinct that fulfilled what the time intrinsically demanded.

The great men in history are those whose own particular aims contain the substantial will that is the will of the World Spirit. The can be called *heroes*, because they have drawn their aim and their vocation not merely from the calm and orderly system that is the sanctified course of things, but rather from a source whose content is hidden and has not yet matured into present existence. This source is the inner Spirit that is as yet hidden beneath the surface; it knocks at the outer world as though that were a shell, and shatters it because that inner Spirit is a kernel that is different from the kernel in the outer world's shell. Thus, these men seem to create from within themselves, and their actions have produced a set of conditions and worldly relations which seem to be only *their* interest, and *their* work.

These heroic individuals, in fulfilling these aims of theirs, had no consciousness of the Idea at all. On the contrary, they were practical and political men. Yet at the same time they were thoughtful men, with insight into what was needed and what was timely: their insight was the very truth of their time and their world—the next species, so to speak, which was already there in the inner source. It was theirs to know it, this universal concept, the necessary next stage of their world—to make this their aim and to put their energy into it. The world-historical men, the heroes of an era, are therefore to be recognized as the insightful ones; their deeds and their words are the best of their time. Great men have worked to satisfy themselves, not others. Whatever they might have learned from others in the way of well-intentioned advice—all this would have been narrow-minded and distorted under the circumstances. For they were the ones who best understood what was right, and from them all the others learned it, and approved their actions, or at least accommodated themselves to them. The advanced Spirit is thus the inner soul of all individuals; but this is an unconscious inwardness which the great men bring to consciousness for them. This is why the others follow these soul-leaders; for they feel the irresistible force of their own spirit coming out in the heroes.

If we take another look at the final destiny of these world-historical individuals who had the calling to manage the affairs of the World Spirit, we find that their destiny was by no means happy. They attained no calm enjoyment, their entire life was toil and trouble; their entire nature was nothing but their master-passion. Once their goal is achieved they fall away like empty shells from the kernel. They die young, like Alexander; they are murdered, like Caesar; they are exiled, like Napoleon to St. Helena. There is a horrible consolation in the fact that these historical men did not achieve what is called happiness—a happiness found only in private life, and under very different external circumstances—and this is a comfort that can be drawn from history by those who need it. But those who need that consolation are also the envious, who resent greatness and eminence, who seek to belittle greatness and to find fault with it. Thus, in modern times it has been demonstrated all too often that princes are not at all happy on their thrones—so that we are not to begrudge them their position, and are to be glad that it is they who are there, not we. The free man, however, is not envious, but gladly recognizes what is great and exalted, and rejoices in it.

It is in the light of these general elements, therefore—elements that constitute the interest and thus the passions of individuals—that these historical men are to be regarded. Men are great for having willed and accomplished something great—not something based on conceit or presumptuousness, but rather something right and necessary. This standpoint excludes the so-called psychological view which best serves the interests of envy, for it explains all actions as coming from some subjective source, great or small, in the individual—some pathological craving for the sake of which all his actions are done, as though there never had been anyone who acted from moral motives.

Alexander of Macedon conquered part of Greece, and then Asia—*therefore* he must have had a *craving* for conquest. Or he acted from a craving for fame, and the supposed proof that this is what drove him is that his actions did bring him fame. What schoolmaster has not demonstrated that Alexander the Great and Julius Caesar were driven by such passions, and that they were therefore immoral? And from this it immediately follows that he, the schoolmaster, is more admirable than they, since he has no such passions—the proof being that *he* has not conquered Asia nor defeated Darius and Porus, but that *he* is willing to live and let live.

These psychologists are particularly fond of latching on to the peculiarities of great historical figures as private persons. A man must eat and drink, he enters into relations with friends and acquaintances, he has feelings and moments of anger. As a familiar saying has it, "No man is a hero to his valet." To this I added—and Goethe repeated it ten years later—"but not because the former is no hero, but because the latter is a valet." He takes off the hero's boots, helps him into bed, knows that he likes his champagne, etc. Served by such psychological valets in historical writing, the historical personage comes off badly; he is degraded, brought down to the valet level, or even a few degrees below the morality of these fine connoisseurs of humanity. Homer's Thersites, who reproaches the kings, is a typical figure for all times. True, Thersites does not always get thumped with a stout stick, as he does in the Homeric era. But envy and egotism—these are the thorns in his flesh; and the undying worm that gnaws at him is the torturing thought that his admirable intentions and criticisms remain altogether ineffectual in the world. One may even take a certain malicious pleasure at the ultimate fate of Thersites.

A world-historical individual is not so circumspect as to want this, that, and the other, and to take account of everything; rather, he commits himself unreservedly to one purpose alone. So it happens that such individuals treat other interests, even sacred ones, in a casual way—a mode of conduct certainly open to moral censure. But so great a figure must necessarily trample on many an innocent flower, crushing much that gets in his way.

The particular interest linked to passion is thus inseparable from the actualization of the universal principle; for the universal is the outcome of the particular and determinate, and from its negation. It is the particular that is involved in the struggle with others, and of which one part is doomed to perish. It is not the universal Idea which involves itself in antithesis and struggle, exposing itself to danger; it remains in the background, and is preserved against attack or injury.

This may be called the *Cunning of Reason*, that it allows the passions to work for it, while what it brings into existence suffers loss and injury. This is the phenomenal world, part of which is negative, part positive. Compared to the universal, the particular is for the most part too slight in importance: individuals are surrendered and sacrificed. The Idea pays the ransom of existence and transience—not out of its own pocket, but with the passions of individuals.

Some might find it acceptable to see individuals sacrificed, along with their aims and fulfillments, consigning their happiness to the realm of chance (to which it belongs), and even to regard individuals altogether under the category of means to an end. Yet there is that aspect of theirs which we must refuse to see in this light, even for the sake of the highest goal, simply because there is that in individuals which is not to be made subordinate, but is something intrinsically eternal and divine. This is *morality, ethics, religious commitment*.* Already when we spoke of the role of individuals in the actualization of the rational goal, we touched upon the subjective aspect, the interests of individuals, their needs and drives, their views and insights—and although we said that this was the formal aspect in them, it has an infinite right to be satisfied. In speaking of a "means", we at first imagine something merely external to the "end" and having no part in it. But in actuality even natural things in general, even the most common lifeless objects used as means must already be such as to be appropriate to their end and must have something in common with it. Humans do not see themselves as the "means" for the goals of Reason in that entirely external sense at all. On the contrary, not only do they use the occasion to satisfy their particular interests whose content is different from that goal, but they also have a part in that rational goal itself; for that very reason they are to be regarded as ends in themselves.

They are not ends in themselves in the merely formal sense, like the world of living things in general—so that the individual life could be subordinated to human life in general, and might justifiably be used as a means to it. On the contrary, humans are ends in themselves with respect to the content of the goal [of Reason]. This determines what we want to exclude from the category of means—morality, ethics, religion. In other words, the human being is an end in himself only by virtue of the divine in him—by virtue of what, from the very outset, was called "Reason", and called "freedom" too, because Reason is self-activating and self-determining. And although we cannot go into the further development of it here, we assert that morality, ethics and religion have their basis and their source in Reason and freedom, so that they are intrinsically exalted above necessity and chance.

But it must be said here that individuals—to the extent that they are aware of their freedom—are responsible for any ethical and religious deterioration, and for the weakening of ethics and religion.

---

* In this translation, *Moralität* is uniformly rendered as "morality" and its cognates; *Sittlichkeit* is rendered as "ethics", "ethical life", or "the ethical"; *Religiosität* is rendered as "religious commitment" or "religiosity". [Translator's note.]

This is the seal of the absolutely high vocation of Man, that he or she knows what is good and what is evil, and that it is for him or her to will either the good or the evil. It is the mark of the human, in other words, to be capable of bearing such responsibility, not only for the evil but also for the good; and responsibility not only for this, that, or another thing, but responsiblity for the good and evil stemming from his or her individual freedom. Animals alone are truly innocent. (It would, however, take an extensive analysis—as extensive as that needed for the analysis of freedom itself—in order to rule out or avoid all the usual misunderstandings involved in saying that what is called "innocence" means ignorance of evil itself.)

When we contemplate the fate that virtue, the ethical, even religion have suffered in history, we must not fall into the litany of lamentation, about how the good and pious often (or even for the most part) fare ill in the world, while the evil and wicked prosper. By the term "prosperity" one may understand a wide variety of things, including wealth, external honors, and the like. But when we speak of such things as though they were intrinsic goals, we still cannot make the so-called prosperity or misfortune of this or that single individual into an element of the rational world-order. To this world-goal there often goes the demand—with more of a justification than any demand for the happiness or the good fortune of individuals—that good, ethical, and righteous goals should find their realization and security in that world-goal, and under its auspices. What makes people morally dissatisfied (and this is a dissatisfaction upon which they pride themselves) is that they do not see the present as measuring up to the goals they hold as right and good. This applies especially to contemporary ideal models of political institutions [*]—thus contrasting the way things *are* with the way they *ought* to be.

Here it is not the particular interest, not the passion, that demands to be satisfied, but rather the demands of Reason, Justice, and Freedom. And once it is furnished with this title, the demand becomes haughty, and it is not only dissatisfied (all too easily) with world conditions, but even rebels against them. To appreciate such feeling and such purposes, one must examine the demands raised,

---

* See Kant's essay, "Perpetual Peace". [Translator's note.]

the dogmatic opinions asserted. At no time so much as in our own have general principles and ideas been raised up with greater pretentiousness. History usually presents itself as a struggle of passions. In our time, although there is no lack of passion, history shows itself (to some) to be predominantly the struggle between justifiable ideas and (to others) to be essentially the struggle of passions and subjective interests that merely pretend to have a higher justification of this kind. In the name of the final destiny of Reason, these pretended demands for justification are taken as absolute goals—in the same way as religion, ethics, morality.

As was said, nothing is more common today than the complaint that the *ideals* raised by fantasy are not being realized, that these glorious dreams are being destroyed by cold actuality. On their life-voyage, these ideals smash up on the rock of hard reality. They can only be subjective, after all; they belong to that individuality of the solitary subject (*Individualität des Einzelnen*) which takes itself for the highest and wisest. Ideals of that sort do not belong here—for, what the individual (*Individuum*) spins out for himself in his isolation (*Einzelheit*) cannot serve as law for the universal reality, just as the world's law is not for the single individual (*einzelnen Individuen*) alone (who may come off much the worse for it).

But by the term "ideal" we also understand the ideal of Reason, of the good, the true. Poets such as Schiller have presented these ideals in very moving and emotional ways, with the feeling of deep sorrow at the fact that they may never be realized. If, on the contrary, we say that universal Reason does manifest itself in the world, then this certainly has nothing to do with any empirical detail—for that can be better or worse, since the elements of contingency, of particularity, receive from the Idea the power to exercise their tremendous authority in that sphere.

There is much to find fault with, therefore, in the details of the world of appearances. This subjective fault-finding—which is concerned only with the detail and its shortcomings, and does not recognize the universal Reason in it—is all too easy. Having the assurance of its good intentions for the well-being of the totality, together with the appearance of good-heartedness, it can give itself airs and make much of itself. It is easier to discern the shortcomings in individuals, in states, in providence, than to see their true significance. For in negative fault-finding one stands above the thing, nobly and with a superior air, without being drawn into it, i.e., without having grasped the thing itself in its positive aspect. Generally, the critic mellows with age; youth is always dissatisfied. That mellowness of age is a ripeness of judgment—which not only accepts the bad, through disinterestedness, but is also led to what is substantial and solid in the matter in question by having been instructed more deeply by the seriousness of life.

The insight to which philosophy ought to lead, therefore (in contrast to what happens to those ideals), is that the real world is as it ought to be, that the truly good, the universal divine Reason is also the power capable of actualizing itself. This good, this Reason—in its most concrete representation—is God. God governs the world: the content of His governance, the fulfillment of His plan, is world history. Philosophy seeks to understand this plan: for only what is fulfilled according to that plan has reality; what is not in accord with it, is but a worthless existence. In the pure light of this divine Idea (which is no mere ideal) the illusion that the world is a mad or foolish happening disappears. Philosophy seeks to know the content, the actuality of the divine Idea, and to justify the despised reality—for Reason is the perception of God's work.

As for the deterioration, the damage, and decline of religious, ethical, and moral aims and conditions in general, we must say this: Although these values are infinite and eternal in their inner essence, their external expressions can take on limited forms, which in their natural interrelatedness subsist under the command of contingency. This is why they are transitory, and exposed to deterioration and damage. Religion and the ethical—like any other inherently universal essences—have the characteristic of being present in the individual soul (according to their concept, and therefore truly), even if they do not have in that soul the advantage of the full extent of culture or of application to fully developed circumstances. The religiosity or the ethics in a limited mode of life—of a shepherd, say, or of a peasant, limited in their concentrated inwardness to a few and altogether simple circumstances of life—has infinite value, the same value as the religiosity and ethics of a cultivated intellect, and of an existence that is rich in the scope of its relations and activities.

This inner center, this simple region of the rights of subjective freedom; the seat of volition, resolution, and action, and of the abstract content of conscience, embracing the responsibility and worth of the individual—all this remains untouched, entirely removed from the loud noise of world history, removed not only from the external and temporal changes, but also from those changes that are entailed by the absolute necessity of the concept of freedom itself. In general, however, there is this point to be noted: that whatever can claim to be noble and grand in the world still has something higher above it. The claim of the World Spirit supersedes all particular claims.

This may suffice in regard to the means used by the World Spirit for the realization of its concept. Simply and abstractly, the "means" is the activity of those in whom Reason is present as their intrinsically substantial essence—though primarily as a still obscure ground, one that is hidden from them. The matter becomes more complex and more difficult, however, when we regard individuals not merely as active, but more concretely, with the more definite content of their religion and ethics—for these factors have a part in Reason, and hence in its absolute rights. Here the bare relation of means-to-end falls away, and the principal points of view that have arisen regarding the bearing of the absolute goal of Spirit upon this aspect of life have been briefly considered.

III. THE STATE AS REALIZATION OF SPIRIT. The third point to be considered is the goal to be achieved by these means, i.e., the form it takes in actuality. We have spoken of "means"; but in the fulfillment of a finite subjective goal there is also a *material* element, which is already there or must be provided for the actualization. On this analogy the question would be: What is the material in which the rational end-goal is to be realized? Again, it is primarily the human subject, human needs, subjectivity in general. The rational comes to existence in human knowing and willing, as its material.

We have considered the subjective will—how it has an aim which is made the truth of a reality, and especially insofar as this is a great world-historical passion. As a subjective will, with limited passions, the human will is dependent; and it can only satisfy its particular aims within the limits of this dependency. Yet the subjective will also has a substantial life of its own, an actuality within which it moves among essences, and has the essential itself as the goal of its existence.

This essential being is itself the union of two wills: the subjective will and the rational will. This is an ethical totality, the *state*. It is the reality wherein the individual has and enjoys his freedom—but only insofar as he knows, believes, and wills the universal. Yet we ought not to understand this as though the subjective will of the individual came to its fulfillment and enjoyment by way of the common or universal will, with the common will serving as a mere means for the individual—as if the individual were to limit his freedom among other individuals, so that this mutual limitation and inconvenience would provide for each some small space for movement. As against this negative concept of freedom,* it is rather law, ethical life, the state (and they alone) that comprise the positive reality and satisfaction of freedom. The freedom which is limited in the state is that of caprice, the freedom that relates to the particularity of individual needs.

The subjective will—passion—is the actuating element, the realizing force [of Reason]. The Idea is the inner source. The State is the externally existing, genuinely ethical life. It is the union of the universal essential will with the subjective will—and this is ethics. The individual, living in this union, has his own ethical life, he has a value consisting in this substantiality alone. Sophocles' Antigone says: "The divine commands are not of yesterday, nor of today—no, they live forever, and no one can say whence they came." The laws of ethics are not accidental, but are the rational itself. The proper goal of the State is to make this substantiality count in the actual doings of human beings and in their convictions, making it present and self-sustaining there.

It is the absolute interest of Reason that this ethical whole should be present. And herein lies the justification and the merit of the heroes who founded states, no matter how crude. In world history we are concerned only with those peoples that have formed states. For we must understand that the State is the realization of freedom, i.e., of the absolute end-goal, and that it exists for its own sake. We must understand, further, that all the value that human beings possess, all of their spiritual reality, they have through the

---

* This is the "negative freedom" Isaiah Berlin discusses in his essay "Two Concepts of Liberty," reprinted in *Four Essays on Liberty* (Oxford: Oxford University Press, 1969). [Translator's note.]

State alone. Their spiritual reality consists in the fact that their essence—rationality—is objectively there for them as knowers, and that that rationality has an immediate objective existence for them. Only in that way is man a consciousness, with an ethical way of life, the legal and ethical life of the State. For the True is, as we said, the union of the universal (or general) will and subjective will; and the universal dimension is in the State's laws, in the universal and rational arrangements.

The State is the divine Idea, as it exists on earth. In this perspective, the State is the precise object of world history in general. It is in the State that freedom attains its objectivity, and lives in the enjoyment of this objectivity. For the law of the State is the objectification of Spirit; it is will in its true form. Only the will that is obedient to the law is free, for it obeys itself and, being self-sufficient, it is free. Insofar as the State, our country, constitutes a community of existence, and insofar as the subjective will of human beings submits to laws, the antithesis between freedom and necessity disappears. The rational is the necessary, the substantiality of a shared existence; and we are free to the extent that we acknowledge it as law, and follow it as the very substance of our being. The objective and the subjective will are then reconciled, as one and the same serene whole.

The ethical life of the State is not of the moral or reflective kind, wherein one's individual conviction rules supreme. This latter is more appropriate to the modern world; the true ethics of antiquity is rooted in the principle of abiding by one's duty. An Athenian citizen did what was required of him as if by instinct. But if I reflect upon the object of my activity, I must have the consciousness that my will has been called upon. Ethical life, however, is the sense of duty (unquestioned, unconscious), the substantial law—a "second nature," as it has rightly been called (since the "first nature" of human beings is our immediate animal being).

The detailed development of the concept of the State is for the philosophy of right to provide—although we must point out that in the legal theories of our time, various errors are current which are taken for established truths and have become prejudices. We will mention just a few, principally those related to the goal of our [philosophical study of] history.

A. *The theory that confronts us first* is the direct contrary to our concept of the State as the actualization of freedom: namely, the view that the human being is free by nature, but that in society and in the state (of which he is necessarily a part) he must limit this natural freedom of his. That the human being is free by nature is entirely correct, in the sense that he is free according to the concept of humanity; but for that very reason man is free only in terms of his implicit destiny (which is there to be fulfilled). The "nature" of a thing always amounts to the same thing as its "concept"; but it is true that the concept of humanity does include the way the human being exists in his merely natural immediate existence.

The theory before us assumes, generally, a "state of nature." Man is represented as possessing natural rights and enjoying the unlimited exercise of his freedom. This assumption is not directly taken for historical fact. There would also be some difficulty, if it were taken seriously, in providing a proof that any such a natural condition existed in the present or anywhere in the past. One can certainly point to the existence of savage conditions, but these are shown to be linked to the passions, to barbarism and acts of violence—and yet these are linked, however primitive they are, to social institutions involving so-called limitations of freedom. The assumption is one of those nebulous images necessarily produced by the theory (i.e., the image of the noble savage) to which it ascribes existence, without historical justification.

What we find such a "state of nature" to be, in its empirical existence, corresponds equally well to the concept of it. Freedom, as the ideal dimension of original nature, does not exist as an original and natural state. On the contrary, it must first be achieved and won, and indeed won through an endless process involving the discipline of knowledge and will. So, the "state of nature" is not an ideal condition, but a condition of injustice, of violence, of untamed natural drives, inhuman acts, and emotions. There is, to be sure, a limitation imposed upon this state of nature by society and the civil state, but it is no more than a limiting of blunt emotions and crude impulses, as well as the limiting of the reflective arbitrariness of caprice and passion. This limitation is part of the process through which the eventual consciousness of freedom and will to be truly free (according to the concept of freedom, i.e., as rational) is first brought forth. According to that concept, freedom involves law and morality, and these are—in and for themselves—universal essences, objects and aims. These must first be found through the activity of self-developing thought, in opposition to sense experience. Then they must be absorbed and incorporated into the primarily sensuous will, even against its natural inclination.

Freedom is forever misunderstood in this way, being known in only a formal, subjective sense, abstracted from its essential objects and aims. This is why the limiting of the impulses, desires, passions that are proper to the particular individual, as such—the limiting of arbitrary caprice—is taken to be a limiting of freedom. On the contrary, such limitation is simply the condition from which emancipation proceeds; and society and the State are the conditions wherein freedom is actualized.

B. There is a second theory to be mentioned, and this denies the general development of [abstract] Right into the form of Law. The *patriarchal* condition (prevailing either in the entire human race, or at least in some single branches of it) is regarded as the situation in which the ethical and emotional element finds its fulfillment, along with the element of [abstract] Right. Only in connection with these ethical and emotional elements [says this theory] can justice be truly exercised in accord with its content. The patriarchal condition is based upon the family relation, in which the absolutely primitive form of ethical life is consciously developed, followed by the higher form in the state. The patriarchal relation is a transitional condition: the family having grown into a tribe or a people, the unifying bond has ceased to be the bond of love and trust, and has become one of service.

Here we must speak primarily of the ethics of family life. The family may be seen as a single person: in that case, its members have either surrendered their personal claims against one another, along with their legal claims, their extended personal interests, and their selfishness (as in the case of parents); or else they have not yet arrived at the point of asserting such claims against one another (as in the case of children, who are initially in that state of nature discussed above). They are therefore immersed in a unity of feeling, of love, of trust and faith in one another. In this union of love, the individual has the consciousness of self in the consciousness of the other; the individual self is externalized, and in this mutual externalization the individual has won self-hood—and each has gained the other's self with his or her own, since each is at one with the other.

The further interests involved in the needs and external concerns of life (along with the internal development of those interests in regard to the children) constitute a common purpose for the family. The spirit of the family (e.g., in the Roman Penates) is as much *one* substantial entity as is the Spirit of a people in their state. In both, ethical life consists in the feeling, the consciousness, and the will—not of the individual personality and its interests, but of the common personality and interests of all the members in general. But in the family this unity is one of feeling, remaining within the limits of the natural order of things. This piety of family-feeling has to be respected to the highest degree by the state. As a result of this family-feeling, the state has, as its members, individuals who are already ethical in themselves (which they would not be as self-interested persons); and as its members they bring to the state its solid foundation, because each one feels himself to be united with the totality. But the extension of the family to a patriarchal whole goes beyond blood-ties (the natural aspect); and outside these ties, individuals must assume the status of [distinct] persons.

If we were to consider the patriarchal relation in its wider scope, we would be led to a discussion of theocracy: the head of the patriarchal tribe is also its priest. Where the family has not yet been distinguished from civil society and the state, the separation of religion from the family has not yet happened either—and insofar as the piety of family-feeling itself remains an inwardness of feeling, it is not likely to happen.

We have considered two aspects of freedom—the objective and the subjective. Now if freedom means that the individuals give their consent, then it is easy to see that only the subjective element is meant. What follows naturally from this principle is that no law can be valid unless everyone agrees to it. And immediately we come to the implication that the minority view must yield to the majority—the greater number decides. But then, as Jean-Jacques Rousseau noted, there is no longer any freedom, since the will of the minority is no longer taken into account. In the Polish parliament, each individual member had to consent before a law was passed—and for the sake of that freedom the state collapsed. *Moreover, it is a false and dangerous assumption that *only* the people possess reason and insight, and know what is right. Any faction of the people can put itself forward as standing for the People. But what really constitutes a state is a matter of trained intelligence, not a matter of "the people."

If the only criterion of political liberty is the principle of the will of the individual—namely, that each individual is to give his or her consent to everything done by or for the state, and that without such unanimous consent no decision can be taken—then there is actually no such thing as an independent *form of government* operating autonomously. Presumably, the only arrangement that would then be needed would be, first, a neutral center (without any will) that would note what seemed (to it) to be the needs of the state, and would communicate its views; and, second, a mechanism for assembling all individuals, and tabulating their votes for the various propositions before them; in that way the decision would be already made.

The state is an abstraction, having its merely general reality in its citizens; but it is actual, and its merely general existence must define itself as an individual will and activity. This creates the need for government and administration in general, involving the selection of individuals to take the helm in political affairs: they must take decisions about these matters, determine how those decisions are to be carried out, and direct the citizens in the implementation of them. Thus, even in a democracy, if the people decide to embark on a war, there must be a general to lead the army.

Only by means of the state-structure does the abstraction that is the state acquire life and actuality—and in any such structure there is a difference between those who command and those who obey. Obedience, however, seems to be inconsistent with freedom—and those who are in command seem to be doing precisely what contradicts the concept of freedom, which is the very basis of the state. If, then, the difference between commanding and obeying is a necessary one, because otherwise nothing would get done (though indeed this seems only a matter of necessity, something ex-

---

* See Rousseau's *Considerations on the Government of Poland* (1770–71). [Translator's note.]

ternal and contrary to freedom abstractly understood), then the institutions of government must at least be such that as few as possible of the citizens have merely to obey, and the authorities have as little arbitrary power as possible. The range within which commanding authority is necessary should be for the people to decide; in its main outline it should be determined by the will of the many or of every individual citizen, for in that way the state, as an actuality and as an individuated unity, will gain its force and strength.

The primary consideration, above all, is the difference between those who govern and those who are governed. The forms of governance have been correctly classified into monarchy, aristocracy, and democracy. Here we must note, however, that monarchy itself can be divided again into despotism and monarchy proper. In all these merely conceptual classifications, it is only the fundamental differences that are emphasized. These are therefore not to be taken as exhausting the concrete possibilities of forms, types, or modes of government. It is significant that the types of government admit of many variations, not only as sub-types of the above, but also as mixtures of these essential types of order, mixtures which are formless, untenable and inconsistent distortions of those forms. In this clash of forms, therefore, the question is: Which is the *best* form of government? That is, through what arrangements, organization, or mechanism of state power is the intrinsic purpose of the state fulfilled most effectively?

Of course, this purpose can be seen in a variety of ways—e.g., as the calm enjoyment of civil life, or as universal happiness. Goals of this kind have resulted in the formulation of so-called ideals of government, including ideals involving the education of princes (Fenelon)* or of the rulers, as the aristocracy in general (Plato).† The main emphasis was on the nature of those who stand at the head of the state— and in ideal accounts of this kind, no thought was given to the content of the state's organic institutions. The question as to the best form of government is often stated not only as though the theory about it is a matter of free subjective conviction, but also as though the actual introduction of one form (as the

---

* Francois Fenelon, *Télémaque* (1694).
† Plato, *Republic*, Books II-III (376e-405b); VII (521c-535a). [Translator's notes.]

one recognized to be best or as a better one) were the consequence of an entirely theoretical decision—as though the type of government were nothing more than a matter of free choice determined by reflection. In this altogether naive sense, the Persian leaders (though not the Persian people) deliberated about what form of government they wished to introduce into Persia. They had conspired to overthrow the false Smerdis and the Magi; and after the success of the conspiracy they deliberated on the form of government because there was no heir to the throne, and Herodotus tells the story of that deliberation with the same naiveté.*

Nowadays, the form of government of a land or a people is not represented as being so entirely dependent on their free choice. The underlying conception of freedom, regarded abstractly, has led to the widespread acceptance of the theory that the *republic* counts as the only just and genuine form of government. And there are many men who—despite the fact that they occupy high posts in monarchical systems of government—are not opposed to the idea of a republic and even support it. Yet they realize that although the republic may be the best of systems, it cannot be instituted everywhere. And so they realize that—people being what they are—we must be content with less freedom; and that under existing circumstances, given that moral condition of the people, the most useful form of government may be monarchy. Even in this view, although the necessity of a certain form of government is seen to be dependent on the condition of a people, that condition itself is regarded only as the result of external contingency. Such a view is based on the intellectually reflective division between the concept and its reality: either the intellect holds to a merely abstract (and hence untrue) concept; or it does not grasp the idea itself; or (what amounts to the same thing in terms of content, though not in formal terms) the intellect lacks a concrete awareness of what a people or a state is.

Further on we shall show that a people's form of government comprises one substance—one spirit—with its religion, its art, and philosophy, or at least with its thoughts and imaginings, its culture in general (not to mention other influences of an external sort, such as the climate, its neighbors, its place in the world). A state is an

---

* Herodotus, *The Persian Wars*, Book III, Ch. 80–83. [Translator's note.]

individual totality, from which it is impossible to isolate all by itself a particular aspect such as its form of government (although that aspect is of the highest importance); no one aspect is to be deliberated upon and voted upon in that isolated form. Not only is the form of government intimately connected with those other spiritual forces and dependent upon them, but the characterization of the entire spiritual individuality, including all its powers, is only one element in the history of the totality: it has been predetermined in the course of that history, and its history comprises the highest sanction of the constitution, as well as its highest necessity.

The first formation of a state is authoritarian and instinctive. Yet even force, obedience, and fear of a despotic ruler already involve some connection of wills. In the primitive state, it is already the case that the particular will of the individuals (*Individuen*) does not count; one's own particularity (*Particularität*) is set aside, and the universal will (*allgemeine Wille*) is what is essential. This unity of the universal and the individual (*Einzelne*) is the Idea itself, which is now present as the state and which goes on to develop itself further. The abstract (although necessary) course in the development of truly independent states, therefore, is that they begin with monarchy (whether it be patriarchal and pastoral or warlike). Then particularity (*Besonderheit*) and individuality (*Einzelnheit*) assert themselves—in aristocracy or democracy. The conclusion of the process is that this particularity is subjected to *one* power, which can be no other than [constitutional] monarchy —such that the particular spheres have their independence apart from it. Thus we must distinguish between a first and a second form of monarchy. This progression is a necessary one, such that each form of government in the sequence is not a matter of choice, but rather is such as to conform to the Spirit of the people.

What is important in deciding on the form of a state, its constitution, is the development of the rational condition, i.e., the political condition as such, the liberation of the conceptual elements— so that the particular powers are separated from one another and become complete in themselves, yet in their very freedom cooperating toward one purpose and being sustained by it; in short, forming an organic whole. Thus the state is freedom subsisting on its own account, rationally self-conscious, and objectively knowing itself to be such. Its objectivity is in the very fact that its elements are not merely present in a set of ideals, but are rather to be found in a characteristic reality. And in their effective self-relation, these elements pass over into that activity whereby the totality, the soul, the individual unity is produced as their result.

The state is the Idea of Spirit in the externalized form of human will and its freedom. It is in the state, therefore, that historical change occurs essentially, and the elements of the Idea are reflected in the state as various political *principles*. The forms of government, in which the world-historical peoples have blossomed, are characteristic of those peoples. Thus the various forms do not present one universal basis of government—as though the differences consisted only in determinate modes of expression and development [of this universal basis]. Rather, there is a difference, here, in the underlying principles themselves.

Accordingly, when we compare the forms of government of ancient world-historical peoples, there is nothing they can tell us regarding the ultimate principle of the state, as a principle that would be applicable to our own time. In the fields of science and art, the matter is quite different: ancient philosophy provides the basis for modern philosophy to such a degree that the ancient is contained in the modern. The relationship that appears, here, is that of an unbroken development of one edifice, whose foundation, walls and roof have remained the same. And in art, that of the Greeks sets the highest standard just as it is. But in regard to the types of government the situation is quite different: the ancient and the modern have no essential principle in common. To be sure, there are abstract definitions and doctrines concerning lawful government, to the effect that intelligence and virtue should rule—these ideas are certainly shared. Yet nothing is more misguided than to look for models among the Greeks, the Romans, or Orientals for the constitutional structures of our own time. From Oriental culture we have fine pictures of patriarchal conditions, paternalistic government, and devotion on the part of peoples; from the Greeks and Romans we have descriptions of popular freedom, where the constitution admitted all citizens to participation in the deliberations and decisions concerning general affairs and laws.

This is the general opinion in our time as well—but with the modification that since our states are so large and the population so multitudinous, the people must express its will, not directly but indirectly, through its representatives, who contribute to decisions concerning public affairs and laws. The so-called representative system of government is the logical form to which we link our image of a free system, and this link has become a firm prejudice. In it, the people are separated from the government. But there is something malicious in this antithesis: it is a trick of bad will, suggesting that the people are the totality of the state after all. Underlying this idea, moreover, is the principle of individuality, the absoluteness of subjective will (which we discussed above).

The main point [against this mistake] is that this freedom, as defined by its concept, is not based on subjective will and caprice, as its principle, but on the insight into the universal will; and that the system of freedom is the free development of its elements. Subjective will is an entirely formal concept, which does not in any way entail *what* it is that is willed. Only the rational will is this universal will, which determines and develops itself in itself, and unfolds its elements as its organic parts. The ancients knew nothing of this "gothic" intellectual architecture of Reason.

Earlier we set up two elements for consideration: the first was the Idea of freedom as the absolute end-goal; the second was the means to that end, the subjective aspect in knowing and willing, with all their vitality, movement, and activity. Then we went on to see the state as the ethical whole and the reality of freedom, and hence as the objective unity of both those preceding elements. For although we have distinguished the two sides for the purpose of our discussion, it must be carefully noted that they cohere together exactly, and that this mutual entailment is to be found in each of the two elements when we examine each separately.

On one hand we have recognized the Idea, in its determinacy, as the freedom that knows and wills itself, and has only itself as its goal. This is the simple concept of Reason—and at the same time it is what we called the subject, self-consciousness, the Spirit as it exists in the world. If, on the other hand, we consider subjectivity itself, we find that the process of subjective knowing and willing is [nothing other than] thinking. But insofar as I thoughtfully know and will, I will the universal object, the substance of what is in and for itself rational.

Thus we see an intrinsic unification of the objective aspect, the concept, with the subjective aspect. The objective existence of this unification is the state, which is therefore the basis and the center of the other concrete aspects of the life of a people—its art, its laws, its ethics, its religion, its science. All spiritual activity has this goal alone, to make itself aware of this unification, i.e., of its freedom.

Among the different forms of this conscious unification [combining the objective and the subjective], *religion* stands at the pinnacle. Here the existing worldly Spirit becomes aware of the absolute Spirit—and in this consciousness of the essence in and for itself, the human will renounces its particular interest. In devotion all this is set aside, and there is no longer any concern with particulars. Through [acts of] sacrifice we express our renunciation of our property, of our will, and of our particular perceptions. The religious concentration of mind appears as feeling, yet it also goes over into meditation: [active] worship is meditation externalized.

In *art* we have the second form of the unification of the objective and the subjective in Spirit. Art enters more into actuality and sense experience than religion does: in its noblest posture, it is there to present not the mind of God, of course, but the outer form of God, and thus the divine and the spiritual as such. Through art, the divine becomes visible: to fantasy and to sight.

The True, however, does not just achieve representation and feeling (as in religion), and the visual (as in art); it also comes to the thinking Spirit—and we thereby arrive at the third form of the unification: *philosophy*, the highest, the freest, and the wisest configuration of Spirit. We can not propose to consider these three configurations here; all we can do is mention them, since they occupy the same ground as does the object of our study, the *state*.

The universal [dimension] that manifests itself in the state and is known in it—the form which is to include all that is—comprises the *culture* of a nation, taken altogether. The specific content, however, which takes on the form of universality and which inheres in the concrete actuality that is the state, is the Spirit of the people itself. The actual state is animated by this Spirit in all its particular affairs, wars, institutions, etc. But man must also know of this Spirit of his, as his own essence, and create for himself the consciousness of his own unity with it, a unity that is fundamental. For we said that the ethical is the union of the subjective and the universal will. Spirit, however, must come to an explicit consciousness of this union, and the center-point of such knowing is *religion*. Art and philosophy are only the different aspects and forms of this same content.

In considering religion, the question is whether it knows the True, the Idea, in its division or in its true unity. As the Idea in its division, [religion knows] God as the abstractly supreme being, the Lord of heaven and earth, above and beyond all else, and excluded from human actuality. As the Idea in its unity, [religion knows] God as the unity of universal and individual (*Einzelne*), since in Him the individual is seen positively as well, in the idea of the Incarnation. Religion is the place wherein a people gives itself the definition of what it holds to be true. The definition comprises everything belonging to the essentiality of the object, and in it the nature of the object is reduced to a simple basic determination, as the mirror of all determinacy—the universal soul of all particular things. Thus the representation of God constitutes the general foundation of a people [i.e., of its conscious unity].

In this aspect, religion stands in the closest connection to the principle of the state. There can be freedom only where individuality (*Individualität*) is recognized as a positive [aspect] of the divine being. But there is a further connection between religion and the state: on the negative side, secular reality is seen as merely temporal, as motivating itself in individual interests (*in einzelnen Interessen*), and therefore as relative and having no justification. Secular reality is justified only insofar as its absolute soul, its principle, is justified absolutely; and it receives this justification only by being recognized as the manifestation of the essence of God. It is for this reason that the state rests upon religion.

In our time we hear this repeated often—that the state rests on religion—and most of the time nothing more is meant than that God-fearing individuals are more inclined and ready to do their duty because obedience to the sovereign and the law is so easily linked to the fear of God. Certainly, the fear of God, by placing the universal aim above the particular individual, can also turn against the latter,* can become fanatical and act against the state, burning its buildings and destroying its institutions. So the received opinion

---

* This is unclear unless we take "the latter" as a mistaken transcription of Hegel's lecture. Obviously, it should read "the former", since it is against the state (the universal) that the said actions are taken. [Translator's note.]

is that the fear of God should be moderated and should be held with a certain coolness, lest it turn against what is supposed to be protected and maintained by it, and overwhelm it in a storm. Religion has within it at least the possibility of doing just that.

Having arrived at the correct conviction that the state rests on religion, religion can take the position that the state is already there, and that in order to maintain the state, religion must be brought in—in buckets and bushels—to be impressed on people's minds. It is entirely correct that people should be trained in religion, but not in something that is not yet there. For when we say that the state is founded on religion, that the state has its roots in religion, then we mean essentially that religion is prior, and that the state has arisen from it and continues to do so. Or, in other words, the state's principles must be regarded as valid in and for themselves; and they can only be so regarded inasmuch as they are acknowledged to be determinations of the divine nature itself. Thus whatever the nature of the shared religion may be, the nature of the state and its structure must agree with it. The State has truly arisen from religion in the sense that the Athenian or the Roman state, for example, was possible only in the context of the specific paganism of these peoples; similarly, a Catholic state will have a spirit and structure that are different from those of a Protestant state.

That call—that urge and drive—to implant religion in the state, could be taken as a cry of fear and distress (as it so often seems to be), expressing the danger that religion is about to disappear from the state or has already done so. But in that case, the situation would be serious, even more serious than the call intends: for in it there is the belief that religion can be implanted and inculcated as a defense against evil. But religion is not at all such an instrument. As an instrument in the production of itself, the self-productive process goes far deeper.

Another and quite opposite foolishness we meet with in our own time is that of trying to invent and institute types of government without taking account of religion. The Catholic religion (although like Protestantism, it is a form of Christianity) does not ascribe to the state the inherent justice and ethical status that lie in the inwardness of the Protestant principle. That sundering of constitutional law from the ethical arises necessarily from the very nature of Catholicism, which does not recognize law and the ethical as independent, as substantial. But these constitutional principles and institutions—once they are torn away from inwardness, from the last sanctuary of conscience, the quiet place where religion resides—do not have an actual [conscious] center, because they remain abstract and indefinite.

Let us now sum up what we have said about the State: The vitality of the State in the individual citizens is what we have called its ethical life. The laws and institutions of the State are the rights of its citizens. Its nature, its soil, its mountains, air, and waters—these are *their* land, their country, their outward property. The history of the state is in their acts, and what their ancestors have achieved belongs to the citizens of today and lives in their memory. All of this is their possession, just as they are possessed by it, for it constitutes their substance, their being.

Their imagination is filled with all this, and their will is the willing of these laws and this country. It is the temporal whole that constitutes one being, the Spirit of one people. To it belong the individual citizens: each individual is the child of his people, and likewise the child of his time (insofar as the state is seen to be in the process of developing). No one is left behind by his time, nor can he overstep it. This spiritual entity is his very own, and he is its representative. It is that context in which he stands, and from which he goes forth. Among the Athenians, Athens had a double meaning: first, it meant the totality of its institutions; but then also the goddess, who displayed the Spirit of the people, its unity.

This Spirit of a people is a *determinate* spirit, and it is also determined by the historic stage of its development, as we have just said. This spirit therefore constitutes the basis and the content of its self-consciousness in the various forms of which we have spoken [i.e., art, religion, and philosophy]. For in its consciousness of itself, Spirit must be objective to itself; and objectivity immediately involves the emergence of differences which subsist as the totality of all the differentiated spheres of objective spirit. In the same way, the soul exists only insofar as it is an organization of its members, which—by taking themselves together in its simple unity—produce the soul. Thus the people is *one* individuality in its essence: in religion it is pictured, worshipped and enjoyed as God in His essence; in art it is displayed in imagery and vision; in philosophy it is recognized and comprehended as thought. Because of the fundamental identity of their substance, their content and object, these configurations stand in an indissoluble unity with the Spirit of the state. The form of the state as we know it can exist only in the context of a definite religion—just as only *this* philosophy and only *this* art can exist in *this* state.

Moreover, the determinate National Spirit is only *one* individual in the course of world history— for world history is the displaying of the divine, the absolute development of Spirit in its highest forms. In this sequence of stages, it attains self-consciousness, which is its truth. The configurations of these stages are the world-historical National Spirits—the determinate shapes of their ethical life, their form of government, their art, religion, and philosophy. The boundless drive of the World Spirit, its irresistible thrust, is toward the realization of these stages—for this articulation of stages, together with their realization, comprise the concept of Spirit.

World history only shows us how the World Spirit comes gradually to the consciousness of truth and the willing of it. This consciousness and will dawns in the Spirit; Spirit finds its main points, and in the end it arrives at full consciousness.

Four
History in its Development

By now we have come to know the abstract characteristics of the nature of Spirit, the means it uses to realize its Idea, and the form that it takes in the complete realization of its existence: the State. What remains to be considered is the *course of world history*.

Abstractly considered, historical change has long been understood in general as involving a progress to something better, something more perfect. Changes in the world of nature—infinitely varied as these might be—reflect nothing more than an eternally repeated cycle. In nature there is nothing new under the sun, so that the many-sided play of natural forms carries with it a certain boredom. Only in the changes that occur in the realm of Spirit is there anything new. This appearing of [novelty in] the spiritual realm lends man a nature altogether different from that which governs merely natural things. In nature, one and the same stable pattern reveals itself, and all change reverts to it. Humanity on the other hand, has an actual capacity for change, and change for the better, a drive toward *perfectibility*.

This dynamic principle of development (which puts all change under law) has not been well received by religions, such as Catholicism, nor by states which assert it as their genuine right to remain static or at least stable. If we do concede the general mutability of worldly things such as states, we might, first, make an exception for our religion, as the religion of truth; and second, it is always possible to ascribe changes, revolutions, and the destruction of legitimate conditions to the ineptitudes, and especially to the stupidity and evil passions of men. Perfectibility, indeed, is something almost as indefinite as the concept of mutability in general—it is without purpose

57

or end, or without a standard for judging change. The notion of what is "better," the more perfect condition at which the "perfectible" is to aim, remains quite indeterminate.

The principle of *development* also implies that there is an inner determination, an implicitly presupposed ground that is to bring itself into existence. In its essence, this formal determination is Spirit, which uses world history as its theater, its property, and the field of its actualization. Spirit does not toss itself about in the external play of chance occurrences; on the contrary, it is that which determines history absolutely, and it stands firm against the chance occurrences which it dominates and exploits for its own purpose.

Development belongs as well to things in the world of organic nature. Their existence does not show itself to be merely passive, and subject to external changes. Rather, theirs is an existence that proceeds from an immutable inner principle—a simple essence, a simple germ at first, which then brings forth differentiations from within, so that it becomes involved with other things. Thus natural organisms live in a continuous process of change which goes over into their opposite, transforming it into the maintenance of the organic principle and its formation. In this way the organic entity produces itself, making itself into what it implicitly is. In its development the organism produces itself in an unmediated way, without opposition or hindrance: nothing can come between the concept and its realization, between the implicitly determinate nature of the seed and the adaptation of its existence thereto.

In the same way, Spirit is only what it makes of itself, and it makes itself into what it already is implicitly.* Yet in the realm of Spirit, things are entirely different [from things in nature]. The transition that is involved in the actualization of Spirit is mediated by consciousness and will. To begin with, human consciousness and will are immersed in their unmediated natural life; their aim and object, at first, is the natural determination as such. But this natural determination comes to be infinitely demanding, strong and rich, because it is animatied by Spirit. Thus Spirit, within its own self, stands in opposition to itself. It must overcome itself as its own

---

* In the German text this sentence comes immediately before the preceding one. [Translator's note.]

truly hostile hindrance. The process of development, so quiescent in the world of nature, is for Spirit a hard and endless struggle against itself. What the Spirit wants is to arrive at the concept of itself; but it itself hides this concept from itself —and it is even proud and filled with joy in this self-estrangement.

Accordingly, the process of development in the realm of Spirit is not the harmless and peaceful progress that it is in the realm of organic life. Rather, it is a severe and unwilling working against itself. Further, it is not a merely *formal* process of self-development in general. Rather, it is the fulfillment of an aim that has a specific *content*. What this aim is we established at the outset: it is Spirit, and indeed Spirit in conformity with its essence, the concept of freedom. This is the fundamental object, and thus the guiding principle of development as well. It is through this principle that the historical development receives its sense and meaning. For instance, Rome itself is the fundamental object in Roman history, and it is that which guides the consideration of all events for Roman historians. But that is because the events have proceeded from this object, and they only make sense in relation to it, for their content is in it.

In world history there are many great periods that have passed, without any apparent notion of progressive development. Their entire accumulation of culture was destroyed, so that everything had to be started again from the beginning, unfortunately, in order to reach one of the regions conquered long ago in that culture—perhaps with the incidental aid of fragments rescued from those old treasures, but with a renewed and immeasurable expenditure of time and energy, and even at the cost of crime and suffering.* But there also are examples of continuing development, of cultural structures and systems richly built up in all aspects, and with their characteristic elements. The merely formalistic conception of development in general can give no preference to one view over the other; nor can it conceptualize the purpose in the decline of those older periods of development. Instead, it must regard progress of this kind, or more especially the regression in it, as a series of disconnected and external contingencies. That formalistic view of development can assess the advances only according to indefinite

---

* It seems probable that Hegel is alluding here to the birth of Egyptology. [Translator's note.]

criteria—ends which are relative, and not absolute, precisely because development as such is the only aim that is taken to be significant. [So much, then, for the merely formal or abstract conception of development. What about the more concrete and absolute view? Here we have a definite aim in sight.]*

In this perspective, world history presents the *stages* in the development of the principle whose *content* is the consciousness of freedom. The more exact determination of these stages, in their general nature, belongs to logic; their concrete nature, however, is for the philosophy of spirit to provide. Here it is enough to say that the first stage is that immersion of Spirit in natural life which we discussed; the second stage is the emergence of Spirit into the consciousness of its freedom. But the Spirit's initial tearing away from nature is incomplete and only partial, because it issues from the immediacy of nature, and is therefore related to it, so that it is still burdened with it as one of its elements. The third stage is the elevation of Spirit out of this still particular form of freedom into its pure universality—into self-consciousness, the feeling of selfhood that is the essence of spirituality. These stages are the fundamental principles of the universal process. But just how each of these stages is itself a process of its own formation and the dialectic of its own transition in its turn—all that must be left to what follows later.

Here we can only point out that Spirit begins from its own infinite possibility, but *only* from the possibility (which contains its absolute content implicitly). This is the purpose and the goal which it attains only as the end result, and which is only then its actuality. The process of history thus appears, in its existence, to be an advance from the imperfect to the more perfect, but one in which the imperfect stage is not to be grasped abstractly or *merely* as that which was imperfect, but rather as that which at the same time has its own opposite within itself—i.e., it has what is called "perfect" within it, as a germ or as the source of its drive. In the same way, the possibility points (at least in thought) to that which is to become actual: more precisely the Aristotelian concept of potency (*dynamis*) is also *potentia* for it is force and power. Thus the imperfect, as its own opposite within itself, is the contradiction which

---

* This short passage in brackets has been added by the translator.

certainly exists, but which is, by the same token, negated (*aufgehoben*) and resolved. This is the drive, the internal impulse of spiritual life, the drive to break through its own shell of naturalness, sensuality, and self-estrangement, in order to arrive at the light of consciousness, its own selfhood.

The topic of how the beginning of history is to be conceived has generally been linked to the image of a "state of nature"—the condition in which perfect freedom and justice are supposed to exist or to have existed. Yet its historical existence was merely an assumption made in the twilight of theorizing reflection. There is a pretension of quite another sort that is quite widespread today. It is different because it is not an assumption proceeding from thought, but is assumed as a historical fact, one that is confirmed by a higher sanction. This pretense concerns the primordial condition of mankind in Paradise, of which the theologians spoke in their characteristic way in an earlier time (asserting, for example, that God spoke to Adam in Hebrew). This view has been taken up again, but it is now made to serve other purposes. The high authority invoked here is that of the biblical account. But on the one hand this account presents the primitive condition only in terms of the few familiar traits; and on the other hand it presents it either as belonging to human nature in general, or (to the extent that Adam is regarded as an individual person, not a type) as manifested and fulfilled only in this one person or the primeval pair.

Yet the biblical account neither justifies us in thinking of an entire people existing historically in that primitive situation; nor does it in any way justify the supposition that this people developed a pure knowledge of God and nature. According to this fiction, nature, in the beginning, stood as a mirror of God's creation and God's truth, open and transparent before the clear eye of man.* There is even the suggestion—although this is left in a vague obscurity—that in this primordial condition man was already in possession of an indefinite but extended knowledge of God's truth, directly revealed. All religions are supposed to have developed (in a historical sense) out of this primordial condition—although they also corrupted and obscured that primordial truth in abortive error

---

* Friedrich von Schlegel, *Philosophy of History* (1829) (Bohn's Standard Library) Vol. I, p. 91. [Translation of author's note.]

and perversity. In all the erroneous mythologies, moreover, there are traces to be seen of that primordial source and of those primitive religious truths. Hence the investigation of the histories of ancient peoples has as its essential concern the task of getting back to the point where fragments of that primitive revelation can be met with in a greater purity. *

We have to thank the interest in these investigations for much that is valuable. Yet such investigation works directly against itself, for it aims only at giving historical verification to what has already been presupposed as historical. The supposed condition of man's knowledge of God; certain kinds of scientific knowledge (e.g., astronomical knowledge that is fancifully attributed to the Hindus); the assertion that this condition prevailed at the very beginning of history, or that the traditions of the various religions began from this knowledge, and developed through a process of degeneration and corruption (like that which is pictured in the crudely conceived system of emanations, as it is called)—all these are presuppositions that have no historical foundation; and as soon as we contrast their arbitrary subjective source with the true concept of history, we know that they can never achieve one.

It is only fitting and proper to philosophic contemplation for us to take up history at the point where rationality begins to enter into worldly existence, not where it is still merely an unrealized possibility; that is to say, history must begin where rationality makes its appearance in consciousness, will, and action. The inorganic exis-

---

* We have to thank this interest for many valuable discoveries in Oriental literature, and for a renewed study of known treasures of ancient Asia—its conditions, mythology, religions, and history. In cultivated Catholic countries, governments have ceased to deny the demands of thought, and have felt the need to associate themselves with learning and philosophy. Abbé Lamennais has made an eloquent and impressive case for the view that the true religion must be universal—i.e., "catholic" in the literal sense—and the oldest; and the Congregation in France has worked zealously and diligently to make such assertions more than merely the pulpit tirades and authoritarian dicta they once were. In particular, attention has been drawn to the religion of Buddha—a god/man—whose religion is enormously widespread. The Indian Trimurti [the Hindu "Trinity": Brahma, Vishnu, Siva], as well as the Chinese abstraction of the Trinity, have been made clearer in

tence of Spirit—the unconscious ignorance of freedom, of good and evil, and hence of laws (or, if you like, the unknowing perfection of it)—is not itself an object of history. The natural (and at the same time religious) ethics is that of family piety. In a natural society, its ethical aspect consists in the fact that the members do not relate to one another as individuals of independent will, or as "persons" [i.e., as having legal rights and claims against one another]. For this reason, the family is implicitly excluded from the development in which history first arises. But when spiritual unity begins to extend beyond this circle of feeling and natural love, and arrives at the consciousness of personality, then a dark inflexible center is present, for which neither nature nor spirit is open and transparent. They become open and transparent only through the further effort of culture, which still has far to go before it can form a will that has become self-aware. Consciousness alone is what is open in this sense— that to which God and anything else can be revealed. Nothing can reveal itself in its truth, and in its intrinsic universality, except to a consciousness that is aware of itself. Freedom is nothing but the knowing and the willing of substantial universal objects such as Right and Law, and the production of a reality that is adequate to them—i.e., the state.

A people may have lived a long life without having arrived at their destination by becoming a state—and they may well have developed a significant culture in some directions. As we said, this *prehistory* lies entirely outside our concern—[no matter] whether a genuine history comes after it, or the people involved never arrived at the formation of a state. It is only some twenty-odd years since

their content. The scholars Abel Remusat and Saint-Martin have undertaken praiseworthy research in Chinese literature, and have branched out into Mongolian and as far as possible into Tibetan literature. On the other hand, Baron von Eckstein, in his journal *Le Catholique*—adopting superficial physical concepts from Germany and imitating Friedrich von Schlegel's manner of interpretation, although in a more clever way—has furthered the cause of this primordial Catholicism. In particular, however, he also gained government support for scholars to journey to the Orient in search of treasures that may still be hidden. These promise to reveal much about the deeper doctrines, and especially about the greater antiquity and sources of Buddhism—thus to promote the cause of Catholicism by these indirect means, however interesting they might be to scholars. [Author's note.]

the great discovery of Sanskrit, with its connection to European languages. This discovery—amounting to a new world—has given us a view of the tie between the Germanic [i.e., European] and the Indian peoples, with as much certainty as can be demanded in such matters. Hence we now know of peoples who had hardly formed a society, much less a state, but who are known to have existed for a long time. And there are others, whose civilized condition must interest us above all, but whose tradition goes back beyond the history of the state's founding; and they must have undergone many changes prior to that epoch. The just-mentioned linguistic connection between peoples so widely separated demonstrates, as an incontestable fact, the dispersion of these peoples from their Asian center, and at the same time the disparate development of cultures that are related by a primeval kinship. This conclusion was not arrived at by means of the favorite method of combining all sorts of circumstances, big and little, and drawing inferences from them—a method that has enriched (and will continue to enrich) history with so many fictions put out as facts. But this great event, with its far-reaching consequences, lies outside history, having happened before history began.

In German, the term for "history" (*Geschichte*) is derived from the verb "to happen" (*geschehen*). Thus the term combines the objective and the subjective sides: it denotes the actual events (in Latin, *res gestae*) as well as the narration of the events (in Latin, *historiam rerum gestarum*). This union of the two meanings must be regarded as something of a higher order than mere chance. We must therefore say that the narration of history is born at the same time as the first actions and events that are properly historical. A shared inner source produces history in both senses at the same time. Family memories and patriarchal traditions have an interest that is confined to the family and tribe. The uniform course of events (in tribal tradition) is not the proper matter for historical recollection. But distinctive deeds or turns of fate may rouse the muse of memory (*Mnemosyne*) to give shape to its images—just as love and religious emotions provoke the imagination into giving form to impulses that had been formless.

It is the state, however, which first presents a subject matter that is entirely appropriate to the prose of history; indeed, the state creates it as it creates itself. Instead of the subjective orders that suffice for the needs of a ruling power at a given moment, a community that is in the process of shaping itself into a state requires rules, laws, universal and universally binding directives. And as it produces them it also produces an intelligent and definite record of (and interest in) actions and events whose results are lasting. Mnemosyne is thereby driven to give enduring remembrance to them, in the interest of the permanent purposes that are characteristic of the state as it forms. Deeper emotions generally—such as love and religious vision, together with their inner imagery—have an [eternal] presence and reward in themselves. The state, however, in the external existence of its rational laws and customs, is only incompletely present. For an integrated understanding of itself it needs a consciousness of the past.

The time periods —whether we think of centuries or of millennia—that have elapsed for peoples before the writing of history, may have been filled with revolutions, migrations, the wildest changes. But these peoples are without an objective history, because they have produced no subjective historical narratives. If the accounts are missing it is not because they have accidentally disappeared, but because they never could have existed. Only in the state, with the consciousness of laws, are there clear actions—and with them the clarity of consciousness having the capability and the need to preserve them. Everyone who begins to become acquainted with the treasures of Indian literature finds it striking that this land—so rich in the most profound spirituality—has no history. In this respect it contrasts most vividly with China, an empire which possesses such excellent historical records, going back to the earliest times.

Not only does India have ancient religious texts and brilliant works of poetry, but ancient codes of law—the very thing that was set down just now as a precondition in the formation of history— and yet it has no history. The organizing impulse that led to social differentiation was immediately ossified into caste distinctions interpreted as determinations of nature. Thus, although the laws concern civil rights, the rights themselves are made to depend on the natural distinctions. They are concerned, above all, with the reciprocal *prerogatives* of these social classes—in terms of higher against lower, and of wrongs rather than rights. As a result, the ethical element is excluded from the splendor of Indian life and from its realms. Due to the unfreedom arising from the natural permanence of the caste system, the cohesion of society is nothing but wild arbitrariness—fleeting activity or rather blind rage—without any goal for progress or development. Hence there is no thoughtful remembrance, no object there for Mnemosyne. And although there is a deeper fantasy, it is still wild; but to be capable of having a history this fantasy would have to have a purpose that relates both to the actual world and to substantial freedom.

Because this is the precondition of history, much has happened without giving rise to history: the rich and immense growth of families into tribes, of tribes into nations; their consequent spread, along with so many complications, wars, revolutions, decline—all occurring with much noise and clamor, although all has remained in effect silent and has passed by stealthily, unnoticed.

A fact established by the study of ancient inscriptions is that the languages spoken by peoples in their crude stage were highly elaborate. Human understanding threw itself into this theoretical field, and developed itself thoroughly and intelligently. [The results are] extended and consistent systems of language that reflect the work of thought as it develops its categories. It is also a fact that with the advance of civilization, and the growth of society and the state, language becomes poorer and cruder as this systematic work of the understanding is worn away. It is a peculiar phenomenon that the progress toward greater spirituality and rationality should neglect that intellectual exactitude and comprehensibility, finding it burdensome and superfluous.

Language is the activity of theoretical intelligence in the true sense, since it is the outward expression of it. Without language, the activities of recollection and imagination are initially just internal utterances.* But this activity of theoretical intelligence, along with its further development and the more concrete events connected with it—the dispersion of peoples, their separation from one another, their intermingling and wandering—all of it remains wrapped in the obscurity of a mute past. These are not the acts of a

---

* Here we have accepted the reading given in Hegel's manuscript as printed by Hoffmeister. Karl Hegel's text reads: "immediate utterances [or manifestations]." [Translator's note.]

will becoming self-conscious, nor of a freedom that is expressing itself in the otherness of a genuinely external actuality. Since they do not participate in this genuine element of freedom, these peoples do not achieve any history, in spite of their linguistic development. The premature growth of language, and the progress and dispersion of nations, have gained significance and interest for concrete historical Reason only in connection with states or with the beginnings of state formation.

After these remarks on the *beginnings* of world history and the prehistory that is excluded from it, we must go on to consider the *course* of history more closely, though only in its formal aspect. The further delineation of its concrete content will be dealt with in the chapter on the division of history.

World history, as we saw, presents the development of consciousness, the development of Spirit's consciousness of its freedom, and the actualization that is produced by that consciousness. This development entails a gradual process, a series of further determinations of freedom, that arise from the concept of world history. The logical nature, and moreover the dialectical nature of the concept in general is that it is self-determining: it posits determinations in itself, then negates them, and thereby gains in this negation (*Aufheben*) an affirmative, richer, and more concrete determination. This necessity, and the necessary series of the purely abstract determinations of the concept, is dealt with in logic. Here we need only make the point that every stage has its own definite characteristic principle, and so it differs from the others.

In history, any such principle is a distinct differentiation of Spirit—the particular Spirit of a People (*Volksgeist*). In this particularity, Spirit expresses in concrete ways all the aspects of its consciousness and will, its entire reality: the shared stamp of its religion, its political system, its ethics, its system of law, its customs, as well as its science, art, and technology. These special characteristics are to be understood in the light of the universal character that is the particular principle of a people. Conversely, that specifically universal character has to be sought in the factual details presented by a people's history.

That a distinct particularity actually constitutes the characteristic principle of a people—this is the aspect which must be taken up empirically, and be demonstrated by historical means.

The performance of this task presupposes not only a practiced faculty of abstraction, but also a close familiarity with the Idea. One must be familiar with the entire circle of its principles on an *a priori* basis, as one might say. Thus—to name the greatest man in this *a priori* mode of cognition—Kepler had to have *a priori* acquaintance with ellipses, cubes, and squares, and with the theory of how they are related, before he could invent—from empirical data—his immortal laws consisting of determinations of those concepts. One who is ignorant of the elementary concepts of that science could no more understand those laws than he could invent them—no matter how long he stared at the heavens and the movements of the stars.

Objections have been raised against the philosophic consideration of a science that regards itself as empirical, objections against the so-called *a priori* approach: importing ideas into the empirical stuff of history, etc. But these objections stem from a similar unfamiliarity with the theoretical structure of the self-development of freedom. Such ideas then appear as something alien, something that has no place in historical objectivity. For one whose personal culture has not made him familiar with pure thought, it certainly is strange, for it is not to be found in the imagination or the understanding shaped by this ignorance of the matter. It is this ignorance that produces the statement that philosophy does not understand sciences such as history. And philosophy must indeed admit that it does not have the sort of understanding that prevails in such sciences, and that it does not operate according to the categories of that kind of understanding. Instead, it proceeds according to the categories of Reason, whereby it knows the true value and status of that understanding. But in the process of scientific understanding as well, it is necessary to separate the essential from the so-called inessential, and to give it proper emphasis. For this to be possible, however, one must be acquainted with what is essential. But what is essential in world history, when it is seen as a totality, is the consciousness of freedom, and the determinations of that consciousness in freedom's development. To direct attention toward this category is to direct it at what is truly essential.

Particular instances are sometimes cited, in order to contradict a universal conception. [Thus, one might point to instances of irrationality to contradict the principle that reason rules the world; or instances of unfreedom to contradict the view that history is the development of freedom.]* But this is usually due, in part, to an inability to grasp and understand theoretical ideas. In natural history, a monstrosity, an unfortunate example of mongrel growth, might be brought in as an instance against the notion of clearly distinguished species and classes. But then we might rightly apply a saying, which is often uttered in a vague sense, that the exception proves the rule. That is to say, it is for the rule to show the conditions in which it applies, and to point to the deficiency, the hybridism in any deviation from the normal.

Nature, in its weakness, cannot maintain its general classes and species against other elementary influences. Thus, for example, we might think of the concrete organization of the human being, and say that a brain and a heart, etc., are essential in order for organic life to go on in a human; and then a wretched abortion might be brought up as a counter-example, something that has a human form (in general or in part), and which was produced in a human body, lived in it and breathed after it was born, but there is no brain in it and no heart. If we imagine such an instance being brought as a counter-example to the concept of the general structure of the human being (using that latter term in only the most superficial sense), then we can certainly say that a real, concrete human being is something different: it must have a brain in its head and a heart in its breast.

Similarly, it may rightly be said that genius, talent, moral virtues and feelings, piety—all can occur anywhere, in all political systems and conditions; and that there are abundant examples of this. If such assertions are meant to deny that these distinctions are important or essential, then thought has become stuck in abstract categories and is disregarding their specific content. Of course, no distinguishing principles for any such specific content are to be found in these abstract categories. The sophisticated mind that adopts formal points of view of this kind, enjoys a vast field for ingenious questions, erudite views, and striking comparisons, and for seemingly profound reflections and declarations—which can become all the more brilliant the vaguer their subject; and they can be

---

* This sentence was inserted by the translator.

varied and renewed over and over, in inverse proportion to the certainty and rationality that results from them.

In this sense, the well-known Indian epics can be compared with those of Homer—and can even be regarded as superior to them, if the wealth of fantasy is taken as an indication of poetic genius. And on the basis of the similarity of some fantastic features of individual deities, one might recognize certain figures of Greek mythology in those of Indian mythology. Along similar lines, Chinese philosophy, by taking the concept of the *One* as its basis, has been held to be the same as the monistic philosophy of the Eleatics and the system of Spinoza. Further, its way of expressing itself in terms of abstract numbers and lines has led some commentators to see Pythagorean as well as Christian elements in Chinese philosophy. Examples of bravery, enduring fortitude, traits of generosity, of self-denial and self-sacrifice—to be found among the most savage as well as the most weak-spirited nations—are taken as sufficient grounds for the view that there is as much public virtue and private morality to be found in these nations as in the most civilized of Christian countries, or even more.

In this regard, doubt has been raised as to whether human beings have become better at all through the progress of history and civilization, whether their morality has improved: i.e., insofar as morality is seen to be based only on subjective intention and insight, on whatever the acting individual sees as right or wrong, good or evil—not on a principle concerning what is right and good, bad and evil, in and for itself (or on the basis of a religion regarded as being true).

We can spare ourselves the trouble of illustrating the bare formalism and error of such a view, and of establishing the true principles of morality (or rather, of ethics) against this false morality. For world history moves on a higher level than that on which morality properly exists. (We shall take morality to refer to private sentiment, the conscience of individuals, their own personal wills and modes of action. These have their own independent value, responsibility, reward or punishment.) Whatever it is that is demanded and achieved by the end-goal of Spirit, in and for itself, whatever it is that Providence does—all this transcends the obligations, the imputation of motives, the demands, etc., that fall upon individuals in regard to their ethical conduct.

There are those who, on ethical grounds and with nobler feeling, have resisted what the progress of the Idea of Spirit has made necessary. They stand higher in moral worth than those whose crime has—in the higher order [of historic Providence]—been turned into a [mere] means to motivate the will toward that higher order. But in upheavals of this sort, both parties generally stand within the same circle of corruptibility; so it is thus only a formal right—abandoned by the living Spirit and by God—that is defended by those who regard themselves as formally justified.

The deeds of the great men who are the individual agents of world history thus appear justified not only in the inner significance (of which they are unaware), but also from the standpoint of world history itself. But seen from this standpoint, moral claims must not be raised against world-historical acts and those who do them, as those claims do not apply here. The litany of private virtues—modesty, humility, love of humanity, charity—must not be raised against them. World history could altogether ignore the circle comprising morality and the oft-mentioned difference between morality and politics. Not only could it abstain from making moral judgments (since the principles involved in world history, and the necessary relations of actions to these principles, are already the judgment in itself). It could also leave individuals entirely out of view and unmentioned. What world history has to record, rather, are the actions of the Spirit of peoples. The *individual* configurations assumed by Spirit in external reality could be left to limited histories, rather than to world history.

The same sort of formalism [as that of the "subjective" morality discussed four paragraphs back] latches on to vague ideas about genius, poetry, and philosophy, and in similar fashion finds them everywhere and in all things. These vague ideas are the products of intellectual reflection. There is a general culture in such generalities, which bring out and designate essential differences with some dexterity, but without getting into the true depth of things; yet it is something formal, in the sense that it aims only at breaking things down into their component parts (regardless of their content) and at grasping them in intellectual definitions and forms. This is not the free universality which must on its own account be made an object of consciousness.

This kind of consciousness—directed at thought itself and at its forms in isolation from all matter—is philosophy, which certainly has general culture as the precondition of its existence. But this general culture is the capacity to take up the given content and endow it with the form of universality, so that it possesses both—form and content—as an inseparable whole. Form and content are so inseparable that a culture may regard its content as merely given, empirical, as "there"—as though thought had no part in it. But in the analysis of an idea into a multitude of ideas, the content is enlarged into an immeasurable abundance. And it is just as much an act of thought (and indeed of the understanding) to take an object which is of itself concrete and rich in content, and make it into a simple idea (such as Earth, Man, or Alexander and Caesar), designated by a single word—as it is to analyze the idea into its parts, to isolate them, and to give those parts particular names.

It follows, therefore, that just as philosophic reflection brings forth the generalities of genius, talent, art, and science, so formal culture—at every stage of intellectual development—not only can but must grow and reach full bloom, when a given stage of development forms itself into a state. On this foundation of civilization the cultural whole advances to intellectual reflection and to forms of universality in every other sphere, just as it does in constitutional law. Civil life, as such, entails the necessity of formal culture and with this rise of the sciences, as well as cultivated poetry and art in general. Everything included under the heading of plastic arts requires (if only in its technological aspect) the shared civilized life of a human community. The poetic art—having less need of external means, and having the voice (the element of Spirit's immediate existence) as its medium—emerges with great boldness and cultured expression, even before a people is united into a civil life. As we remarked earlier, this is because language reaches a high level of intellectual development long before civilization.

Philosophy, too, must make its appearance in the life of the state. For the process through which a content becomes the stuff of culture is the proper form of thought, as we just said; and so philosophy (which is only the consciousness of this form itself, the thinking of thinking) has the characteristic material that it needs for its own edifice available in the general culture. In the development of the state itself, there must be periods when spirits of a nobler nature are driven to flee from the present into ideal regions, in order to find there the reconciliation with themselves that they can no longer enjoy in the divided world. At such times, the reflective understanding attacks everything holy and profound that has been naively embedded in the religion, the laws and customs of a people—it flattens and dissipates everything in abstract godless generalities. At such a time, thought is driven to become thinking reason, in order to attempt the restoration [of substantial truth] in its own element, out of the corruption to which it has been brought.

Thus, among all world-historical peoples we are certain to find the art of poetry, the plastic arts, science, and philosophy. They differ, however, not only in style and general direction, but even more in content; and this content affects the highest mode of difference—that of the rationality involved. It is of no help when some pretentious aesthetic criticism insists that what ought to please us in these things is not the material aspect, the substantial aspect of content—but rather that it is the beautiful form as such, the greatness of the imagination and the like, which is the real goal of fine art; and that it is this that ought to be regarded and enjoyed by persons of liberal feeling and cultivated mind. Sound common sense, however, does not admit such abstractions and does not take to works of that kind. For instance, one might put the Indian epics on a par with the Homeric ones, for any number of such formal characteristics: the greatness of invention and imagination, the vitality of imagery and feeling, the beauty of diction. But there still remains the infinite difference of content. This, then, is what is substantial here, along with the interest of Reason, which aims directly at the consciousness of the concept of freedom and its imprinting in the individual citizens.

Not only is there a classic form; there is also a classic content. Moreover, in a work of art we see form and content so closely bound together, that the form can be classic only insofar as the content is classic. In the case of a fantastic content which does not set limits for itself —and it is the rational in itself that imposes measure and aim—the form also loses all measure and form, or else it becomes petty and painfully restricted. Similarly, in the equating of those philosophical systems that we mentioned earlier, what is overlooked is the one important point: namely, the nature of the unity and difference to be found in the Chinese, the Eleatic, and the Spinozistic philosophies. Is that unity to be grasped as abstract or as concrete, and does the concreteness go so far as to become a unity in itself, so that it is Spirit? Putting these philosophies on a par just shows that the critic is only aware of the abstract unity; and whoever offers a judgment based on such an equation is ignorant of just what constitutes the interest of philosophy.

But there are also spheres of culture that remain the same, despite all the variety in their substantive content (in art, science, and philosophy). This cultural variety concerns the thinking Reason and freedom—the freedom which is the self-consciousness of Reason and which shares the same root with thought. Just as it is only the human being that thinks, and not the animal, so it is only the human being that has freedom; and then only because he is capable of thinking. His [thinking] consciousness entails this: that the individual comprehends himself as a person; i.e., that he grasps himself as intrinsically universal in his very singularity, as capable of abstraction, of renouncing all particularity, and hence as being inherently infinite. Thus, spheres that are outside this individual understanding provide a shared basis for those substantive cultural differences. Morality itself, which is so closely dependent on the individual consciousness of freedom, can be very pure despite the absence of that subjective consciousness: that is, insofar as it expresses only the general duties and rights of the agent as objective commandments; or, also, insofar as it remains something merely negative, that involves the merely formal elevation [of consciousness], and the surrender of the sensuous and of all sensuous motives.

Chinese morality has received the greatest praise and appreciative recognition from Europeans committed to Christian morality, ever since they first became acquainted with Chinese morality and with the writings of Confucius. In the same way there is recognition of the sublimity with which Indian religion and poetry (of the higher sort), and especially its philosophy, declare and demand that the sensuous must be set aside and sacrificed. Yet both these nations, it must be said, are entirely lacking in the essential consciousness of the concept of personal freedom. To the Chinese, their moral laws are like the laws of nature, expressed as external positive commands, compulsory rights and duties, or rules of courtesy toward one another. What is missing is the element of freedom, through which alone the substantive determinations of Reason become moral conviction in the individual. Morality, for them, is a matter for the state to rule on, and is handled by government officials and the courts. Their works on the topic (those which are not books of law but are rather directed at the subjective will and disposition) read like the moral writings of the Stoics: they offer a series of commandments which are necessary to the goal of happiness, so that the individual can arbitrarily decide to follow them or not; and, as in the Stoic moralists, there is the representation of the abstract subject, the sage, who stands as the culmination of Chinese moral doctrine. And in the Indian teaching about the renunciation of sensuality, the renunciation of desires and earthly interests, the aim and end is not affirmative ethical freedom, but rather the negating of consciousness—in mental and even physical lifelessness.

The concrete Spirit of a people—that is what we must come to know directly. And since it is Spirit it can only be known in spiritual terms, or through thought. It is Spirit alone that asserts itself in all the actions and tendencies of a people; it brings itself to its own actualization, to self-enjoyment and self-knowledge, for it is concerned with the production of itself. The highest achievement of Spirit, however, is to know itself, to bring itself not only to the sight of itself but also to the thought of itself. This it must accomplish and will accomplish. But this accomplishment of Spirit is at the same time its decline—to make way for another Spirit to come forward, another world-historical people, another epoch of world history. This transition and connection leads us to the interconnectedness of the whole, to the concept of world history as such. This we must now examine more closely, and give a presentation of it.

World history in general is thus the unfolding of Spirit in *time*, as nature is the unfolding of the Idea in *space*.

If we then cast a glance at world history in general, we see an enormous picture of actions and changes, of infinitely varied formations of peoples, states, individuals—in restless succession. Everything that can enter the mind of man and interest him—all feeling for the good, the beautiful, the great—everything has its part to play. On all sides, aims which we recognize are taken up and pursued, aims whose accomplishment we wish for, hope for, fear for. In all these events and chance occurrences we see human activity and suffering uppermost; everywhere there is something we appropriate and make our own, thus turning our interest toward or against a thing. At times we are drawn to something by beauty, by freedom and the wealth of possibilities; at other times by the energy through which even vice can make itself significant. At times we see the more comprehensive mass of a general interest advancing slowly, only to see it utterly destroyed by an infinite complex of trifling circumstances. Then again we see tremendous forces producing small results, and enormous results following from seemingly insignificant causes. But everywhere the most variegated crush of events draws us into its sphere of interest; and when one such interest disappears, another immediately takes its place.

This restless succession of individuals and peoples that are here for a time and then disappear suggests one general thought, one category above all, that of universally prevalent *change*. And what leads us to apprehend this change in its negative aspect is the sight of the ruins of some vanished splendor. What traveler, amidst the ruins of Carthage, Palmyra, Persepolis, or Rome, has not been led to contemplate the transiency of empires and of men, and to sorrow at a once vigorous and rich life that is now gone? This is not a sorrow that dwells upon personal losses and the transiency of one's own aims; instead, it is a disinterested sorrow at the decline of a radiant and cultured life.

But the next consideration that is linked to that of change is that this decline is at the same time the emergence of new life—for although life leads to death, death also leads to life. This is a great thought which the Orientals have grasped, and it is perhaps the highest thought in their metaphysics. This thought relates to the individual in the idea of the soul's reincarnation. But in relation to natural life in general, the idea is more familiar in the image of the Phoenix, continually preparing its own funeral pyre and being consumed on it, so that a new, rejuvenated, and fresh life continually arises from its ashes. This image, however, is only Asiatic—it is Eastern, not Western. When Spirit consumes the outer shell of its existence, it does not merely go over into another shell, and it does not merely arise rejuvenated from the ashes of its embodiment; instead, it emerges as a purer Spirit, exalted and transfigured. It does, indeed, go against itself, and consume its own existence. But in so doing, it reworks that existence, so that whatever went before is the material for what comes after, as its labor elevates it into a new form.

If we consider Spirit in this aspect—recognizing that its changes are not merely rejuvenating transitions returning to the same form, but rather elaborations of its own self, through which it multiplies the material for its own endeavors—then we can see how Spirit tests itself in any number of directions, exercising and enjoying itself in an inexhaustible variety of ways. Each of the creations, in which Spirit has already achieved satisfaction, becomes raw material for it once more, and so presents a new challenge for elaboration. Thus the abstract thought of change transforms itself into the thought of Spirit, manifesting, developing, and perfecting its powers in all aspects of its full realization. We experience all the powers it possesses in itself, in the variety of its products and configurations. In the joy of this activity, Spirit has only itself to deal with. It is, of course, involved with the conditions of nature, internal as well as external, but it does not merely encounter opposition and obstacles in them; it will often see its ventures fail because of natural conditions, and succumb to the resulting complications, through its own fault or nature's. But it perishes then through its own vocation and functioning—and thus it still presents the spectacle of having proven itself to be spiritual activity.

It is the essence of Spirit to *act*, to make itself explicitly into what it already is implicitly—to be its own deed, and its own work. Thus it becomes the object of its own attention, so that its own existence is there for it to be conscious of. That is the case with the Spirit of a people too: it is a definite Spirit, one that builds itself up into an entire world, which subsists and persists, here and now, in its religion, its forms of worship, its customs, its form of government and political laws, in the entire scope of its institutions, its deeds and events. This is its work—it is what this people *is*. A people is what its deeds are. Every Englishman will say: We are the ones who go down to the sea in ships; ours is the commerce of the world, ours is India and its wealth; we are the ones who have a parliament, a jury system, etc.

The relation of the individual to the Spirit of a people is such that he appropriates to himself this substantive being, so that it becomes his character and capability, enabling him to be *something* in the world. The individual discovers the being of his people as a firm world, already there, into which he must incorporate himself. The

Spirit of a people itself rejoices and finds its satisfaction in this work, its world.

A people is ethical, virtuous, and strong, insofar as it brings forth what it wills, defending what it does against external force in the work of objectifying itself. The dichotomy between what a people is in itself (subjectively) in its inner purpose and essence, and what it actually is, is then removed: it is at home and self-sufficient, and it is there for itself (objectively). But then this activity of Spirit is no longer needed, because it has what it wants: a people can still do much in peace and war, internally and externally, but the living substantial soul is, as it were, no longer active; the fundamental, or the highest, interest has now gone out of life—for there is interest only where there is opposition.

The people lives (at this stage) like an individual passing from manhood to old age, enjoying himself in being exactly what he wanted to be and could be. If his imagination once went beyond this, he gave up any such aim because it did not suit reality, and he restricted his aim accordingly. *Habit* (like the watch wound up and going by itself) is what brings on natural death. Habit is activity without opposition: only formal duration is left to it, in which the fullness and depth of one's purpose no longer needs to be given voice—one leads an external sensory existence, so to speak, no longer immersed in the object. In this way, individuals as well as peoples die a natural death. And although a people may go on existing, it is an existence without life or interest, without need of its institutions because the need has been satisfied—a political nullity and boredom. For a truly universal interest to arise, the Spirit of a people must come to the point of wanting something new. But where could this new thing or purpose come from? It would be as if the people had a higher, more universal idea of itself, going beyond its present principle—but in this there would be a new and more determinate principle, a new Spirit.

Such a new principle does indeed come into the Spirit of a people which has attained its actualization and fulfillment. That Spirit does not die a merely natural death, since it is not merely a single individual but is a universal spiritual life. What appears in it as a natural death is closer to being national suicide. The reason why it is different from the case of the single natural individual is that the Spirit of a people exists as a *genus* or type, i.e., as a universal, and so its negative dimension comes to exist within it, in its very universality. A people can die a violent death only when it is already naturally dead within itself—as, for example, in the case of the German Imperial cities of the Holy Roman Empire, or the German Imperial system. The universal Spirit does not die a merely natural death at all. It does not simply subside into the senility of habit. On the contrary, because it is the Spirit of a people and a part of world history, it also comes to know what its special work is, and so to think of itself in that light. For it is only world-historical at all insofar as a *universal* principle is seated in its basic element, its basic goal. Only to that extent is the work which such a Spirit produces an ethical and political organization. If [natural] desires are what drive the peoples to their actions, then the actions vanish without a trace—or rather, the traces left are in corruption and ruin.

Thus (according to Greek mythology) it was *Chronos* (Time) who ruled first—in that golden age, without ethical works—and what was produced, the children of Time, were devoured by time. Only Zeus—from whose head Athene was born, and whose circle included Apollo and the Muses—conquered Time and set a goal to its passing. Zeus is the political God who produced an ethical work, the state.

The universality of a work is itself entailed in its element, as a determinate dimension, the dimension of thought. Unless thought is its basis, the work has no objectivity. The highest point in the culture of a people, then, is this thought—the thought of its life and condition, its laws, its system of rights and its ethical way of life, all seen in a scientific light. For in this unity (of the inner and the outer dimensions: inner thought and outer culture) there is that inner-most unity in which Spirit can be at home with itself. The concern of Spirit in its work is to have itself as its own object. But it is only by thinking itself that Spirit has itself as object in its most essential nature.

At the level of thought, therefore, Spirit knows its own principles, the universal dimension of its actions. But at the same time this work of thought, as universal, is different in form from the actual workings of culture and from the effective life through which this work of culture has come into being. This dichotomy involves an ideal existence as well as a real existence. For example, if we want to arrive at a general representation and thought of what the ancient Greeks were, we shall find it in Sophocles and Aristophanes, in Thucydides and Plato. These are the individuals in whom the Greek Spirit has apprehended itself in representation and thought. This is the deeper satisfaction of Spirit, although it is also ideal and thus distinct from what is effectively real.

In such a time, therefore, we necessarily see a people finding satisfaction in the idea of virtue: and its talk about virtue is in part associated with actual virtue itself; but in part the talk of virtue takes the place of it. But just because it *is* universal, the simple universal thought knows how to relate to what is particular, and what has not been reflected upon—faith, trust, ethical custom—and to make thought about them lead to reflection about itself and its own simple immediacy. In that way it shows up the unreflected life for its limited content. For, on the one hand, that simple thought can give reasons for denying its obligations; and on the other, it can also demand to be given reasons that cohere logically with universal thinking—and not finding them, it seeks to make out that duty itself is unfounded and shaky.

In this time of critical enlightenment there comes the isolation of individuals from one another, and from the community as a whole; the individual's destructive selfishness and vanity break in with the search for personal advantage and satisfaction at the expense of the whole. But in addition to this subjectivity of content, the divisive inner principle is also subjective in form: egoism and corruption through the gratification of unstrung passions and self-interest.

Thus Zeus set a limit to the devouring activity of Time and stayed its transience by establishing something of lasting value—the State. Yet Zeus and his race were themselves devoured by that productive principle itself: the principle of thought and of cognition, the principle of knowledge, of reasoning, of insight based on reasons and on the demand for reasons [all of which undermined customary obedience to the gods in the course of history].*

Time is the negative element in the sensory world: thought is this same negativity; but it is the innermost infinite form itself wherein everything that exists is, in principle, dissolved—and chiefly the finite being, the determinate form. But the existent is in principle determined as objective; and therefore it appears as something

---

* The phrase in brackets was added by the translator.

given and immediate, as authority. It subsists either as finite and limited in its content, or as a limit for the thinking subject and its infinite reflection in itself.

But first we must note that the life that proceeds from death is only another individual life once more; and if the species is seen as the substantial element in this alternation, then the death of the individual is a regression of the species into individuality. In this light the preservation of the species is only in the uniform repetition of the same mode of existence.

And secondly, we must note that cognition—which is the thoughtful apprehension of being—is the source and birthplace of a new form, a higher form whose principle is in part to preserve, in part to transfigure its material. This is because thought is the universal, the species which does not die but retains its self-identity. The determinate form of Spirit does not merely pass away naturally in time, but is negated (*aufgehoben*) in the self-activating, self-reflecting activity of self-consciousness. Since this negation is an activity of thought, it is (at one and the same time) a preservation and a transfiguration.

Thus on one hand, Spirit negates the reality, the subsistence of whatever *it is*; and on the other hand it gains the essence, the thought, the universal concept of that which *it merely was*. Its principle is no longer the immediate content and purpose that it previously was, but is its own very essence.

The result of this process, therefore, is that in objectifying itself and thinking of its own being, the Spirit first of all destroys the particular determinacy of its being, and secondly it grasps its own universality, and by doing that it gives a new determination to its principle. In this way, the substantial determinacy of this National Spirit has transformed itself—i.e., its principle has risen to another and in fact a higher principle.

To have the thought of this transition, and to be acquainted with it, is the most important point for our grasp of history and our comprehension of it. An individual, as a single entity, goes through various stages of development and remains that individual. The same is true of a people: it, too, goes through a series of stages, until it reaches the one which is the universal stage of its Spirit. In this last stage lies the inner necessity, the conceptual necessity, of the change. This, then, is the very soul, the distinguishing element, in the philosophic grasp of history: namely, that the transitional or final stage is what defines *that* people.*

In essence, Spirit is the result of its own activity: its activity is the transcending of what is immediately there, by negating it and returning into itself. We can compare it with the seed of a plant: the plant begins with the seed, but the seed is also the result of the plant's entire life. Yet the vulnerability of life is shown when the beginning and the result fall asunder. The same is true in the life of individuals and of peoples. The life of a people brings a certain fruit to ripeness— since its activity aims at fulfilling its nascent principle. Yet this fruit does not fall back into the womb of the people that produced and matured it. On the contrary, it becomes a bitter draught for this people: because of its unquenchable thirst for it, the people cannot let the cup pass from it, even though the drinking means its own destruction—and this leads to the rise of a new principle.

We have already explained the end-goal of this progression. The principles of the various National Spirits, progressing in a necessary series of stages, are themselves only phases of the one universal Spirit: through them, that World Spirit elevates and completes itself in history, into a self-comprehending *totality*.

Because we are concerned only with the idea of Spirit—and we regard the whole of world history as nothing more than the manifestation of Spirit—when we go over the past, however extensive it may be, we are really concerned only with the *present*. This is because philosophy, which occupies itself with the True, is concerned with what is eternally present. Nothing in the past is lost to philosophy: the Idea is ever present, Spirit is immortal, i.e., Spirit is not the past, nor the non-existent future, but is an essential *now*.

This is as much as to say that the present form of Spirit contains all the earlier stages within itself. Certainly, these stages have unfolded themselves successively and independently; yet what Spirit is, it has always implicitly been. The difference lies only in the degree of development of this implicit nature. The life of the ever-present Spirit is a cycle of stages: on one hand [for philosophy] the stages co-exist side by side; on the other hand [for history] they appear as past. But the phases which Spirit seems to have left behind it, it also possesses in the depth of its present.

---

* This last phrase was added by the translator.

Five
The Geographical Basis of History (excerpt)

The Spirit of a people has now been seen in its universality as an ethical whole, acting as a single individual. In contrast to this perspective, the natural coherence of Spirit is something external. But insofar as we must regard that natural coherence as the ground upon which the Spirit is active, it is an essential and necessary basis for its activity. We began with the assertion that in world history the idea of Spirit appears in the actual world as a series of external forms, each of which manifests itself as an actually existing people. That existence falls not only in time but in space as well, in the manner of any natural being. And the particular principle which every world-historical people carries in itself it has within it as a natural characteristic as well.

By dressing itself thus in this natural garment, Spirit allows its particular configurations to go their separate ways—for separation is the form of naturalness. In the first place, these natural differences must also be regarded as offering the particular possibilities out of which the Spirit of a people emerges—and thus they provide the geographical basis for that emergence. It is not our task to get to know that ground as an external locale, but only as the natural type of the locality which corresponds to the type and character of the people that is the child of such ground. This national character is the very manner and mode in which these people make their appearance in world history, taking their special position and place in it.

Nature ought not to be rated either too high or too low in all this. The mild Ionian sky surely contributed much to the charm of Homeric poetry; yet that sky alone could produce no Homers after

83

the one, and if it could such poets would not always be coming forth, for under Turkish domination no such bards arose.

To begin with, we must take note of the natural factors that must be excluded, once and for all, from our consideration of world history. For example, we could never find the ground for world-historical peoples in the torrid zone or in the frigid zone. This is because the awakening consciousness is initially involved only in the natural environment; and every development of that consciousness is a reflection of Spirit back into itself, out of the immediacy of nature (and extremes of heat and cold would not permit such an escape). Thus the element of nature enters into the individuation of humanity. It is the first standpoint out of which humanity can wring a certain freedom for itself—and this liberation must not be overburdened by the power of nature.

In contrast to Spirit, nature is a quantitative power; and its force must not be so great as to be overpowering all by itself. In the outer zones, the human being can achieve no freedom of movement—since heat and cold are forces too powerful there to allow the human spirit to build a world for itself. Aristotle said: "When pressing needs are satisfied, the human being turns to what is higher and more general."*But in the extreme zones, those needs can never cease, and can never be evaded: the human being is constantly compelled to give his attention to nature, to the glowing rays of the sun, and the icy frost.

The true theater of world history is therefore the temperate zone—or rather its northern part, since the earth presents itself in continents and has, as the Greeks said, a broad breast. In the southern part, on the other hand, it divides itself into many parts and disperses itself in many directions. The same difference is evident in the products of nature: the north has many species of animals and plants, but with common characteristics; in the south, where the land is divided into many points, natural forms are more individualized in contrast to one another.

The world is divided into the *Old* and the *New*—and the latter is called "new" because America and Australia became known to us comparatively recently. But these are new not only in a relative sense

---

* *Metaphysics*, I:2 (982b23).

but new altogether, in respect of their whole physical and spiritual make-up. We are not concerned with their geological antiquity. I will not deny the New World the honor of having risen from the seas together with the Old World, at the time of the earth's creation. And yet the archipelago between South America and Asia shows a certain physical immaturity: most of the islands are merely a covering of earth over rocks, as it were; they have welled up from the bottomless depths and have a character of late origin. New Holland (Australia) shows a geography no less immature—for if we go from the English possessions deeper into the country, we discover immense rivers that have not yet dug a riverbed for themselves but empty out into marshes.

About America and its original culture, namely that of Mexico and Peru, we do have some information, but only to the effect that this culture was entirely immersed in Nature, and that it had to go under at the approach of Spirit. America has always shown itself to be physically and spiritually impotent—and it still does so—for after the Europeans landed, the natives gradually perished at the mere breath of European activity. In the separate states of North America all the citizens are of European descent; the old inhabitants could not intermingle with them but were pushed back. There are some arts that the natives certainly adopted from the Europeans, including the drinking of whiskey, which had a destructive effect on them.

In the south the natives were treated far more violently, and were exploited for hard work, for which their strength was hardly adequate. The main character of the native Americans is a placidity, a lassitude, a humble and cringing submissiveness toward a Creole, and even more toward a European—and it will take a long time for the Europeans to produce any feeling of self-confidence in them. The inferiority of these individuals in every respect, even in regard to size, is very apparent. Only the extremely southern tribes, in Patagonia, are stronger by nature, but they are still in the natural condition of barbarism and savagery.

As we know, the Jesuits and other Catholic clergy established a state in Paraguay, as well as monasteries in Mexico and California. Since they wished to accustom the Indians to European culture and morals, they mingled with them, and prescribed their duties to them for the day as though they were under age. Lazy though they were, the Indians bowed to the authority of the fathers. These prescriptions—and at midnight a bell had to remind them of their matrimonial duties—have quite properly led to further needs, which are the mainsprings of human activity in general.

The weakness of the native American physique was a major reason for bringing Negroes to America, through whose strength the necessary work could be done. The Negroes are far more receptive to European culture than the Indians. An English traveller has provided examples of Negroes becoming gifted ministers, physicians, etc. (It was a Negro who first discovered the use of quinine.) On the other hand, this Englishman knew of only one single native American who was sufficiently developed to engage in study, but he soon died in consequence of an overindulgence in whiskey. Their weakness of physique is accompanied by a lack in the instruments of progress—horses and iron—which is the main reason why the native Americans were conquered.

Since the original nation has vanished, or nearly so, the effective population comes for the most part from Europe. And what happens in America has its origins in Europe. Europe has thrown its surplus population to America—in much the same way that in the Imperial cities (where the guilds were dominant and became exclusive and inflexible) many people fled to other towns that were not so restricted and where the burden of taxes was not so great. That was how many of the major cities came to have subsidiary towns associated with them: Hamburg has Altona, Frankfurt has Offenbach, Nuremberg has Fürth, and Geneva has Carouge.

North America relates itself to Europe in the same subsidiary role. Many Englishmen have settled there, where there are no burdens or taxes, and where the accumulation of European means and European skill have succeeded in winning something from the broad and still empty soil. This emigration does indeed offer many advantages, since the emigrants have rid themselves of much that restricted their activity at home, and they bring with them the treasure of European self-awareness along with their abilities. For those who are ready to work hard, and have not found the opportunity in Europe, America has opened a new theater of action.

As we know, America is divided into two parts, joined by a narrow isthmus—although this has not led to a commercial bond between them. Instead, the two parts are very decisively divided. North America, when we approach it from the east, shows a broad coastline. Behind this there is a mountain range: the Blue Mountains or Appalachians; and further north there are the Alleghenies. Streams flow from them to irrigate the coastal lands, which has been most advantageous for the American free states that were first established in this region. Behind that mountain range the St. Lawrence river flows from south to north, linking a series of enormous lakes; the northern colonies of Canada lie along this river. Farther west we encounter the basin of the vast Mississippi, with the riverbeds of the Missouri and the Ohio whose waters it receives, after which it empties into the Gulf of Mexico.

On the western side of this region there is another long mountain range which runs through Mexico and the isthmus of Panama; and under the name of the Andes or Cordilleras it cuts off the entire western side of South America. The coastal border thus formed is narrower and offers fewer advantages than the coastline of North America. On that western side of South America lie Peru and Chile. On the eastern side, flowing east there are the enormous Orinoco and Amazon rivers. These form great valleys, which are not suitable for cultivation since they are merely wide steppes. The Rio de la Plata flows south; its tributaries originate in part in the Cordilleras, and in part in the northern mountain range separating the Amazon region from its own. To the region of the Rio de la Plata belong Brazil and the Spanish republics. Colombia is the northernmost coastal land of South America. At the western side of Colombia, the Magdalena empties into the Caribbean.

Except in Brazil, republics have generally arisen in South America as in North America. If we now compare South America (including Mexico) with North America, we can perceive an astounding contrast.

In North America we see prosperity growing from an increase in industry and population, from civil order and firm freedom. The entire federation comprises but one state, and has its various political centers. In South America, on the other hand, the republics rest only on military force. Their entire history is a continuing upheaval: federated states fall asunder, others reunite, and all these transformations are established through military revolutions. The more specific differences between the two parts of America show them moving in two opposed directions. There is a political difference on one hand and a religious one on the other:

South America, where the Spaniards settled and asserted their hegemony, is Catholic; North America, although a land of different denominations, is fundamentally Protestant. The further divergence is that [politically] South America was conquered, North America was colonized. The Spaniards took possession of South America in order to rule and to become rich, by means of political offices as well as extortion. Dependent upon a very remote mother country, their arbitrariness found greater scope; and through force, ability, and confidence, they gained a great ascendancy over the Indians. The North American states, on the contrary, were entirely colonized, and by Europeans. Since, in England, the Puritans, Episcopalians, and Catholics were involved in constant conflict, and first one, then the other had the upper hand, many people emigrated in order to seek freedom of religion in foreign parts.

It was industrious Europeans who devoted themselves to agriculture, to raising tobacco and cotton. The general attention was soon directed to labor. The substance of the totality was comprised of the needs, peace, civil rights, security, freedom, and a community that arose from the aggregation of atomic individuals, so that the state was only an external institution, set up for the protection of property. From the Protestant religion came the trust of individuals in one another, their reliance on their convictions—for in the Protestant church religious works are the concern of one's entire life and activity. Among Catholics, on the other hand, there is no basis for such trust, because in secular matters only force governs and voluntary subjection—and the forms called constitutions are merely emergency remedies, and offer no protection against mistrust.

In further comparing North America with Europe, we find in the former the perennial example of a republican system of government. There is an inner unity in it, for there is a president as head of state who is elected for only four years (as security against any possible monarchical ambitions). The general protection of property and the almost total absence of taxes are continually commended. This shows us the basic character of the society: it is marked by the private person's striving for acquisition and profit and by the predominance of a private interest which devotes itself to the community for personal benefit alone. There is, to be sure, a legal system, and a formal code of laws; but this legality has nothing to do with integrity—and so the American merchants have the bad reputation of cheating with the protection of the law.

We said that the Protestant church evokes in its members the essential principle of confidence in others; but this gives importance to the element of feeling, which may lead to every sort of capriciousness. From this standpoint, if every person may have his own world-outlook, he may also have his own religion. This explains the proliferation of sects, to the point of sheer craziness: many of the sects have a form of worship that involves convulsive motion as well as the most sensual excesses. This total arbitrariness is such that the various communities hire and fire ministers as they please: the church is not something that subsists independently, in and for itself, with a substantial spirituality of its own and an external establishment; instead, religious matters are handled according to the particular views of the congregation. In North America the wildest freedom of imagination prevails. What is missing is the religious unity found in European states, where deviations are limited to a few denominations.

As for the political situation in North America, its general goal has not yet been settled upon as something fixed. There is as yet no firm coherence in the political structure. A genuine state and a genuine government arise only when there is a difference in classes, with great wealth and great poverty—so that a great mass of people can no longer satisfy its needs as it used to do. But America is not yet approaching such tension—for, to a great extent, there is the constant outlet of further colonization open to it, with a constant stream of settlers into the plains of the Mississippi. In this way the main source of discontent is removed, thereby guaranteeing the continuation of the present civil condition.

It is impossible, therefore, to compare the individual states in the United States with European countries, for in Europe there is no such natural outflow of population, despite all the emigration: if there had still been great forests in Germany, the French Revolution would certainly not have flared up. Only after the immeasurable spaces of America are filled, and the population of this civil society is pressed together, only then will it be possible to compare North America to Europe. In the meantime, North America is still in the condition of being able to add to the land under cultivation. Only when, as in Europe, the increase in the farming population is checked by lack of available land, only then will the population press back upon itself in cities, with their industry and trade, to build a compact system of civil society and so develop the need for an organized state.

The United States has no neighboring states to mistrust, as the European states do, against which they must maintain a standing army. Canada and Mexico are nothing to be feared by the United States; and England has learned, through the experience of the last fifty years, that a free America is more useful to her than the America that depended on her. In the American war of independence, the militias of the separate states showed themselves to be as brave as the Dutch in their revolution against the Spanish Philip. But in general, where independence is not at stake, there is less force exerted; hence the American militias withstood the English less successfully in 1814.

America is therefore the land of the future. In the time to come, the center of world-historical importance will be revealed there—perhaps in a conflict between North and South America. It is the land of longing for all those who are weary of the historic arsenal that is old Europe. Napoleon is reported to have said, "Cette vieille Europe m'ennuie." America has to separate itself from the ground upon which the world's history has taken place until now. What has taken place in America so far is a mere echo of the Old World, and the expression of an alien vitality. As a land of the future it does not concern us here: for in the historical perspective we are concerned with what has been and with what is; and in regard to philosophy our concern is neither with what was nor with what is yet to be, but with what *is* as eternal Reason—and that is enough to keep us occupied.

Let us therefore set the New World aside, along with its associated dreams, and return to the Old World, the theater of world history.

We must first draw attention to natural elements and natural determinants. Just as America is divided into two parts, so the Old World is divided by the Mediterranean. But the three continents around it are related to one another and comprise a totality. The Mediterranean is a means of communication between them; indeed, rivers and seas are not to be seen as divisive but as unifying: e.g., England and Brittany, Norway and Denmark, Sweden and Livonia were united by the waterways between them. The Mediterranean, therefore, is the center of world history. Greece lies here, the focal point of history. In [what is nominally] Syria there is Jerusalem, the center of Judaism and of Christianity. To the southeast are Mecca and Medina, the source of Islam. To the west are Delphi and Athens; and farther west there is Rome, with Alexandria and Carthage on the south side of the sea. Thus the Mediterranean is the heart of the Old World, that which conditions it and gives it its life. Without it we could not imagine world history —any more than we could think of Rome or Athens without the forum where all things converged. The Far East is outside the course of world history—as is northern Europe, which entered world history history only later and had no part in that history in ancient times. Ancient history limited itself throughout to the countries around the Mediterranean. Julius Caesar's crossing the Alps—the conquest of Gaul and the relation the Germans thereby entered into with the Roman Empire—therefore marks an epoch in world history, which thus crosses the Alps as well. Eastern Asia and the land beyond the Alps are the extremities of that mobile center around the Mediterranean—the beginning and the end of world history [in ancient times], its rise and its decline. . . .

Six
The Division of History

The course of history in general was presented in the geographical survey. The Sun, the Light, rises in the East. Light, however, is simple self-relatedness: and the light that is universal in itself is also a self-enclosed subject, in the sun.

The scene has often been pictured in which a blind person suddenly gains sight, sees the dawn, the growing Light, and then the Sun as it blazes up. At first, in his complete amazement, he forgets himself utterly, in this pure clarity. But when the sun has fully risen, his amazement is lessened; he looks at the objects around him, and from them he goes on to see his own inwardness, and then the relation of outer to inner. He proceeds from inactive contemplation to activity: by evening he has constructed some sort of building, by the use of his own inner sun—and when he contemplates it in the evening, he values it higher than that first external sun. For he now stands in relation to his own creative spirit and hence in a relation of freedom [because that spirit is related to itself]. If we keep this image before us, we can see the course of world history in it, the great daily work of the Spirit.

World history goes from East to West: as Asia is the beginning of world history, so Europe is simply its end. In world history there is an absolute East, *par excellence* (whereas the geographical term "east" is in itself entirely relative); for although the earth is a sphere, history makes no circle around that sphere. On the contrary, it has a definite East which is Asia. It is here that the external physical sun comes up, to sink in the West: and for that same reason it is in the West that the inner Sun of self-consciousness rises, shedding a higher brilliance.

World history is the process by which the uncontrolled natural will is disciplined in the direction of the universal, the direction of subjective freedom. The East knew (and knows) only that *One* person is free; the Greek and Roman world knew that *Some* are free; the Germanic world of Europe knows that *All* are free [as persons]. Accordingly, the first political form to be seen in world history is that of Despotism, to be followed in turn by Democracy and Aristocracy, and finally by Monarchy.

To understand this division we must note the following: the state is the universal spiritual life, to which the individuals who are born into it relate with trust and habitual acceptance, so that they have their essence and their actuality in it. This being so, we must ask above all else whether their actual life involves them in the unity of unreflective habit and custom, or whether the individuals are persons who reflect, as independent subjects. In this connection, we must make the distinction between substantive (i.e., objective) freedom and subjective freedom. Substantive freedom is the intrinsic rationality that is implicit in the will of a people, which then develops itself within the state. But at this stage of Reason's development, we do not as yet have individual insight and personal will, i.e., subjective freedom. This only defines itself in the individual [consciousness], where it constitutes the individual's reflection in his own conscience. In the merely substantive (or objective) freedom, on the other hand, the commandments and laws are [seen as] intrinsically fixed, and the individual subjects relate to them in total servitude. These laws need not correspond to the will of the individual; and thus the subjects are like children who obey their parents but are without will or insight of their own.

But when subjective freedom arises, and the person goes from the external reality back down into his own mind, the antithesis of reflection makes its entrance, carrying within it the negating of reality. Thus the reflective withdrawal from the surrounding world already constitutes an implicit antithesis: on one side there is God and the divine; on the other side the human subject as particular. In the unmediated and unreflective consciousness of the East, the two sides are undivided. The substantive world does distinguish itself from the individual, but the antithesis is not yet present to his mind.

The first stage of world history, therefore, is that of the *Oriental World*. Its basis is in the unmediated consciousness, the substantive spirituality to which the subjective will relates itself primarily in terms of faith, trust, and obedience. In its political life we find a realized rational freedom that develops, without advancing to subjective freedom. This is the childhood stage of history.

The splendid structures of the Oriental empires form substantial configurations in which all the categories of rationality are present—but in such a way that the human subjects remain merely incidental. The subjects revolve around a center, the ruler, who stands at the head like a patriarch, though not as a despot in the sense of imperial Rome. It is his task to see that the substance of custom is maintained, and to uphold the essential commandments that are already established. That which in our world belongs to the sphere of subjective freedom proceeds there from the universal totality. The splendor of the Oriental vision is the One Individual, as the substantial being to which everything belongs, so that no other subject can distinguish itself as individual and reflect upon itself in its subjective freedom. All the wealth of fantasy and nature is appropriated to that substantial being, in whom the subjective freedom [of all individuals] is immersed—so that their status is not in themselves but in that absolute being. All the elements of the state, including subjectivity, are certainly there, but they are not as yet reconciled with the substantial being. For outside the One Power, before which nothing can constitute itself independently, there is nothing but horrible despotism that sweeps over everything destructively. We therefore see wild hordes breaking forth from the highlands, falling upon these countries, and either devastating them or settling in them and giving up their wild life; but in all cases they are dispersed without a trace in the substantial culture.

This substantiality—because it has failed to take up its antithesis into itself and overcome it—splits directly into two elements. On the one side we see duration, stability; we see empires of *space*, as it were—an unhistorical history [i.e., a history without development in time]—as, for example, in China, with its state based on the family relation and on a paternal government. This government maintains the institution of the totality through providential care, with its admonitions, punishment, and disciplinary actions. It is an altogether prosaic realm, because in it the antithesis of form (in regard to infinitude and ideality) has not yet arisen. On the other side, this spatial durability is countered by the form of *time*: the states, without changing in themselves or in principle, undergo endless change with regard to each other; they are ceaselessly in conflict, which soon brings them to ruin.

In this turn outward, toward strife and struggle, a first hint of the principle of individuality enters —but it comes in an unconscious and merely natural universality: it is the Light that is not yet the light of the personal soul. Here, too, history is predominantly un-historical, for it is merely the repetition of the same majestic demise. The new element—through acts of bravery, prowess, and generos-ity—has come to replace the previous splendor; yet it undergoes the same cycle of decline and fall. So the fall is not genuine, because in all this restless change there is no progress.

At this point history passes over to central Asia, but only in externals, without connection to what went before. If we continue with the comparison of history to human growth, we can say that this is the boyhood stage of history, no longer behaving with the calm and trust of childhood, but rather in a rowdy and aggressive way.

The *Greek World* may then be compared to the period of ado-lescence, for here we see individualities being formed. This is the *second* main principle in world history. Just as in Asia, ethical custom is the principle; but in Greece it is the ethical life that is impressed on individuality, so that it signifies the free volition of individuals. Here, then, we have the union of ethical custom with the subjective will. This is the realm of Beautiful Freedom. Its Idea is combined with plastic form: it is not yet there for itself as an abstraction, but is directly bound up with the real—just as in a work of fine art the sensible matter carries the imprint and expression of the spiritual.

Accordingly, this is the realm of true harmony—the world of the most charming but evanescent and quickly fading blossom: not yet a conscious morality, but a spontaneously ethical life in which the will of the individual stands firm upon the unmediated custom and habit that prescribes what is right and lawful. The individual is thus in a naive unity with the universal aim of society. That which, in the Orient, is divided into two extremes—into the substantive being, as such, and the individuality which grinds itself down against it—is here brought together. But the union of these divided principles is only an *immediate* one and for that reason it is also the highest contradiction in itself. For this *beautiful* ethos has not yet been wrung out in the struggle of subjective freedom, a freedom reborn; the ethos has not yet been raised up, pure, to the free subjectivity of ethical life.

The third stage of world history is the realm of abstract universality: this is the *Roman World*, the hard work of history's manhood. The mature man does not act with a despotic arbitrariness, nor according to his own caprice (however attractive that caprice may be); instead, he works for the common good, in which the individual is submerged, attaining his own ends only in what is shared. The state begins to emerge in an abstract way, and to work toward a goal of its own. Individuals have a share in this end, but their part is not yet an exhaustive and concrete one. Free individuals are sacrificed to the rigid demands of the common goal, to which they must surrender in their service of the abstract universal.

The Roman world is no longer a world of individuals in the way that the Athenian polis was. Here there is no joy and cheer, but only hard and bitter work. The common interest is detached from that of individuals, although in working for it they gain an abstract, formal universality for themselves. The universal end subjugates individuals; they must surrender themselves to it. But in return they receive a universal version of themselves: the status of persons. They become legal *personae*, having a private status.

In the same sense in which individuals are incorporated into the abstract concept of the person, the "individuals" that are independent nations will have to experience this fate as well: that is to say, their concrete form will be crushed by this universality, the Roman state, and they will be incorporated into the greater mass. By incorporating these different cultures, Rome becomes a pantheon of all gods and all things spiritual—although these gods and their spirituality do not retain their characteristic vitality.

The development of this world has two significant sides to it. On one hand, it has an express and declared antithesis within itself, an antithesis based on reflection, or upon abstract universality itself: that is, the Roman world displays within itself the struggle of that very antithesis [i.e., between universality and individuality]. The necessary outcome of all this is that an arbitrary individuality eventually gets the upper hand over the abstract universality. Rome passes into the utterly contingent and thoroughly worldly power of *one overlord*, the emperor. Originally there is the antithesis between the common good of the state (as the abstract universal) and the abstract person. But then, in the course of history, the element of personality becomes predominant; the community then begins to break up into its component atoms, so that it is only held together by means of external power. And then the subjective force of sovereign domination comes forward, as though summoned to this task. For abstract legality cannot be concretely real in the individual, and his life is not genuinely organized around compliance with the law; and inasmuch as abstract legality has come to power, this power is merely arbitrary, as the contingent subjectivity of one mover, one ruler. And then the individual subject seeks consolation for his lost freedom through the development of private right. This is the purely *worldly* reconciliation of the antithesis.

There is also a *spiritual* reconciliation (which is the second side to the development of the Roman world). With the fragmentation of the outer political world, held together only by external force, the pain of the despotism begins to be felt. And the spirit, driven back into its innermost depths, abandons the world that has lost its gods. Spirit then looks to itself for the reconciliation that it needs. Now there begins the life of its inwardness, a fulfilled concrete inwardness, which at the same time possesses a substantiality that is not rooted in outer experience. In the inwardness of the soul, therefore, there arises that spiritual reconciliation, in the fact that the individual personality is purified and transfigured into universality, or into its own implicitly universal subjectivity—transfigured into divine personality. Now the merely secular world is more readily opposed by the spiritual; it is the world of those who know themselves in their own subjectivity, and know that inwardness as their very essence, the world of the actual Spirit.

With this we enter the fourth [stage] of world history, that of the medieval *Germanic World*—history's old age (if we continue the comparison to the cycle of aging in the individual). In nature, old age is weakness; but the old age of the Spirit is its complete ripeness, in which Spirit returns to unity with itself, but as Spirit.

This world begins with the reconciliation that has occurred in Christianity. But this is a fulfillment that is only *implicit*, not fully present in the external world. Accordingly, its beginning is really in the enormous antithesis between the spiritual/religious principle within, and the barbarian reality outside. For to begin with, Spirit itself, as the consciousness of an inner world, is still abstract. Consequently, the secular world is given over to arbitrariness and brutality. At first this barbarism is opposed by the Mohammedan principle, the enlightenment of the oriental world. This develops later and more quickly than Christianity—which needed all of eight centuries before it grew into a worldly form [with Charlemagne]. The principle of the Germanic world became a concrete reality only through the Germanic nations.

The antithesis—between the spiritual principle in the ecclesiastical world and the brutal barbarism in the secular world—is present here as well. The secular world *ought* to conform to the spiritual, but that "ought" contains the recognition that in fact it does not: at first, the mere worldly power must disappear in the face of the ecclesiastical authority; yet ecclesiastical authority, by immersing itself in secular power, loses its spiritual character and force. Through this corruption of the spiritual aspect—i.e., the Church—there emerges a higher form of rational thought: Spirit, having once again been forced back into itself, produces its work in the form of thought, and becomes capable of realizing the principle of rationality from the principle of secularity alone.

That is how it comes about that the realm of thought is brought to birth in actuality through the efficacy of universal determinants which have the principle of Spirit as their basis. The antitheses of Church and State disappear. Spirit now finds itself in the secular world, and builds up that world as an implicitly (*in sich*) organic outward being. The State is no longer inferior to the Church, and no longer subordinated to it. The Church retains no priority; spirituality is no longer foreign to the State. Freedom has now found the tools with which to realize its concept, its truth, in the world.

This is the goal of world history—and we have now to traverse, in detail, the long road which we have presented here only in summary. But the length of time is something entirely relative, whereas Spirit belongs to the dimension of eternity and has no actual length.

Appendix
From Hegel's *Philosophy of Right*

WORLD HISTORY

341. *Universal Spirit* comes into existence through a variety of elements: in art it is through the element of vision and image; in religion it is through feeling and representational thinking; in philosophy it is through thought pure and free. In world history it is through the element of spiritual actuality in its entire scope of internal and external expression. World history is a court of judgment— because in its implicit and explicit *universality*, the *particular* is present only as *ideal* (whether it be the Roman Penates, civil society, or the different national spirits in all their diversity). And the activity of Spirit in this element has to make this plain.

342. Moreover, world history does not just render a verdict of might—i.e., it is not the abstract and non-rational necessity of a blind fate. On the contrary—since Spirit is implicitly and explicitly Reason, and becomes explicit to itself only in knowledge—world history is the necessary development of the elements of Reason out of the concept of Spirit's freedom alone, along with the self-consciousness and freedom of Spirit. It is the display and *actualization* of the universal Spirit.

343. Spirit's history is its *act*. Spirit is only what it does, and its act is to make itself the object of its own consciousness, to apprehend itself as Spirit, explaining itself to itself. This self-apprehension is Spirit's very being and principle; and the *fulfillment* of this apprehension is at one and the same time the externalization of Spirit and

99

the transition beyond it. To say it in formal terms, we can speak of our apprehending that apprehension anew; and then the return of Spirit into itself after its externalization is Spirit at a higher stage than the initial apprehension.

[Remark:] The question that arises here is that of the *perfectibility* of mankind—as discussed, for example, in Lessing's *Education of the Human Race* (1780). Those who have argued for such perfectibility have a notion of the human spirit: that it is in man's nature to have "Know Thyself" as a law of his *being*; and that to the extent that he grasps what *he is*, he has risen to a higher form than that which constituted his mere being, earlier. But to those who reject this thought, "Spirit" has remained an empty word—just as history has remained, for them, a superficial play of *accidental*, "merely human" strivings and passions (as they are called). Even if these critics speak of history in terms of *Providence* and its *Plan*, and thus express a faith in a higher power, the plan of Providence remains an empty idea for them, since they expressly declare that it is unknowable and incomprehensible.

344. In this activity of the World Spirit, states, nations and individuals arise with their *particular determinate principle*. This principle is displayed and actualized in their form of government and in the entire range of their conditions. These states, nations, and individuals are aware of all this, and are deeply committed to the interests involved. Yet at the same time they are the unconscious tools and organs of the World Spirit in its deep activity, wherein these forms pass away, while the Spirit implicitly and explicitly prepares and works out its own transition to its next higher stage.

345. The concepts of justice and virtue; wrongdoing, force, and vice; talents and their achievements; passions, great and small; guilt and innocence; grandeur in individual and national life; independence, happiness and unhappiness for states and single individuals—all these have their distinct meaning and value in the sphere of conscious actuality. In that sphere they are judged and find their justification (however incomplete it may be). World history falls outside these viewpoints. In it, the necessary element of the Idea of the World Spirit is its *present* stage; and this receives its *absolute* legitimation in history. And the nation which expresses that Idea in its own achievements receives its fulfillment, happiness, and fame.

346. History is the configuration of Spirit in the form of what happens, i.e., in the form of immediate natural actuality. For this reason, the stages of its development are out there as *immediate natural principles*. And these principles, because they are natural, are a multitude of independent units, so that only *one* of them pertains to any *one* nation. This is its *geographic* and *anthropological* existence.

347. The nation—to which such an instance of the Idea pertains as a *natural* principle—is entrusted with implementing it as the World Spirit progresses in developing its self-consciousness. This nation is predominant in world history for this epoch—*and only once can it be predominant* and *epoch-making in history*. (See paragraph 346) This nation has an absolute right as the vehicle of the World Spirit in the present stage of its development. Against it, the spirits of other nations have no rights—and they, along with those whose epoch has passed, do not count at that time in world history.

[Remark:] The specific history of a world-historical nation comprises, on the one hand, the development of its principle from its infantile condition in the husk, to the time when it blossoms into its free ethical self-consciousness, and it forces its way into universal history. But on the other hand it also comprises the period of that nation's decline and fall—for that is how the emergence of a higher principle is marked upon it as the negating of its own. This signifies the transition of Spirit to that higher principle, and therefore the passing of world history to *another* nation. The declining nation has by then lost its absolute interest; and even if it adopts the higher principle for itself as something positive, this is not something immanently vital for it. It may lose its independence; or it may drag on as a particular state or part of a group of states, involving itself, according to circumstances, in various enterprises at home or wars abroad.

348. At the actual point of all actions, including world-historical ones, *individuals* are the agents that give subjectivity to what is substantial. They are the vitalizing force behind the substantial deed of the World Spirit, and are thus directly identical with it, although its aim and object is hidden from them. (See paragraph 344) For this they receive no honor or gratitude from their contemporary world, nor from the public opinion of the later world—but their share at the hands of that public opinion is *undying fame* as the formal subjective agents of those deeds.

349. At its beginning, a nation is not yet a state. The transition from a family, a horde, a tribe, a multitude, etc., to the condition of being a state—this constitutes the *formal* realization of the Idea in general, in that nation. A nation is, *implicitly*, an ethical substance. But without the formal condition of statehood it lacks a universal and universally valid objectification in laws as its conscious characteristics—and therefore it is not recognized, either by itself or by others. Without objective legality and rationality explicitly established (by means of government), a nation's independence is merely formal, and is not yet sovereignty.

[Remark:] Even in the ordinary view of things, no one calls a patriarchal condition a government, or a nation in this condition a state, or its independence sovereignty. Prior to actual history, therefore, we have either a condition of dull innocence, without all interest, or the bravery of formal struggle for recognition and revenge.

350. It is the absolute right of the Idea to manifest itself in legal determinations and objective institutions, beginning with laws of marriage and agriculture. Whether that actualization takes the form of divine legislation and favor, or of force and wrongdoing— this right is the *right of heroes* to establish states.

351. In the same light, it happens that civilized nations regard and treat other nations as barbarian when these others lag behind and so lack the substantial elements of statehood. (Thus cattle-raising people might regard a nation of huntsmen as barbarians, while an agricultural people might regard both as barbarian, etc.) The civilized nation is aware of the disparity in rights, between its own and those of barbarian peoples, whose independence they regard and treat as something merely formal and lacking all foundation.

[Remark:] In the wars and quarrels that arise in these circumstances, what makes them significant for world history is that they are struggles for recognition related to a specific cultural value. [Thus nomadic herdsmen have a different concept of the land from that held by crop-growers, etc.]

352. The different concrete ideas, which are the spirits of various peoples, have their truth and determinacy in the concrete Idea which is *absolute universality*: the World Spirit. Around its throne they stand as executives of its actualization, and as witnesses and ornaments to its grandeur. As Spirit, its only activity is to know itself in absolute terms—and in that way to free its consciousness from the form of natural immediacy, and to come to itself. Hence the *principles* of the various configurations of this self-consciousness, in the course of its liberation, are the world-historical realms, of which there are four:

353. In the *first*, or as an *immediate revelation*, the World Spirit has the form of *substantial* Spirit as its principle: the identity wherein individuality remains sunk in its essence, and unjustified on its own account (*für sich*).

The *second* principle is this substantial Spirit in its knowing, so that this substance is its positive content, but it is also conscious of itself. This *being-for-self* is the living form of Spirit—the beautiful ethical individuality. [This is an individuality combining the Beautiful and the Good as primary values (in Greek: *kalokagathia*).]

The *third* principle is the inward deepening of this knowing self-consciousness, to the point of *abstract universality*, and thus to the point of Spirit's infinite opposition to the objective world which has abandoned spirituality in the process.

The principle of the *fourth* configuration is the reversal of this opposition by Spirit: by going into its own inwardness for its truth as well as its own concrete essence, it finally comes to be at home in objectivity and reconciled to it. In thus returning to the earlier substantiality, Spirit has *returned from its infinite opposition*. Spirit now creates and knows its truth as its own thought, and as a world of lawlike actuality.

354. In accordance with these four principles, there are *four* world-historical realms: the Oriental, the Greek, the Roman, and the Germanic.

355. A. *The Oriental World.* This first realm is the substantial world which is emerging from a natural patriarchal totality. In the perspective of this world, which is inwardly undivided, the worldly government is a theocracy; the ruler is a high priest or is even God himself; the state structure and legislation are at the same time religion—just as the religious and moral commandments, or rather customs, are state decrees. In the splendor of this totality, the individual personality has no rights and is suppressed. External nature is directly divine or is God's ornament. The history of the actual world is poetry. Various distinctions develop between classes of people, according to the different aspects of custom, government and state; and these distinctions, operating by simple custom in place of laws, become ponderous, elaborate and superstitious ceremonies. The contingencies of personal power, of arbitrary rule, and of class differences, take on the natural rigidity of castes. The Oriental state, therefore, is alive only in the outward movement of conquest, or in elemental frenzy and devastation. Inner calm occurs only in private life, sunk into weakness and exhaustion.

[*Remark* omitted here.]

356. B. *The Greek World.* Here we have cultural life which still possesses the substantial unity of the finite and the infinite—but only as a mysterious foundation, repressed into an obscured memory, in cult practices carried on in caves, and in images retained by tradition. This background—gradually emerging out of self-differentiating Spirit into individual spirituality, and rebirth in the full daylight of knowing—is moderated and transfigured into beauty and the ethical life of freedom and happiness. It is therefore in this sort of world that we see the principle of personal individuality arising, although it is still not fully autonomous but is kept within its own ideal unity instead [e.g., the individual identifies with the city.] As a result of this inadequate individuation, the [Greek] totality falls apart into a group of individual national spirits on the one hand [e.g., Athens, Sparta, Corinth, etc.]; and, on the other hand, the ultimate resolution of the will is not yet placed in the subjectivity of independent self-consciousness but in a higher external power [e.g., Alexander]; the satisfaction of particular needs, moreover, is not yet a task accepted by free men but is rather relegated to a class of slaves.

357. C. *The Roman World.* Here the process of social differentiation is carried to the point where ethical life is absolutely torn asunder into its extremes: [private life versus public life], *personal* self-consciousness against *abstract universality*. This opposition begins with the antithesis between the substantive outlook of an aristocratic class and the principle of free personality in its democratic form. On the aristocratic side it deteriorates into superstition and the assertion of cold, greedy force; the democratic side sinks into the depravity of a rabble. The dissolution of the social totality ends with universal misfortune and the death of ethical life. National individualities die off and fade into the unity of a Pantheon [i.e., with the deification of emperors]. All individuals are degraded to the sta-

tus of private persons, as *equals* having formal rights, and are held together by nothing more than abstract self-will driven to monstrous extremes.

358. D. *The Germanic World.* Spirit has thus inflicted injury on itself and its world—followed by the infinite grief for the Crucified God, for which the Jewish people was held in readiness. Out of all this, the Spirit driven back into itself, grasps the absolute *turning point* in the extremity of its absolute *negativity*: the *infinite positivity* of its own inwardness, the principle which asserts the unity of the divine and the human natures. This reconciliation (of divine and human) as the objective truth and freedom—that appears within self-consciousness and subjectivity—is a reconciliation entrusted to the northern principle of the Germanic peoples to fulfill.

359. In its inwardness, the principle is still abstract. Existing in the inner sense as faith, hope and love, it reconciles and resolves all antitheses. The principle unfolds its content, elevating it to actuality and self-conscious rationality—to a secular realm that proceeds from the heart, from loyalty and the fellowship of free men. In the subjectivity of its source, that *secular* realm is also a realm of crude arbitrariness and barbarous custom. It stands opposed to the world beyond, an *intellectual* realm—whose content is certainly that truth of its Spirit; but since this Spirit still does not *think*, that intellectual realm remains veiled in barbarous imagery. And as spiritual power over the actual heart and mind, this other-worldly realm acts against it as an unfree [i.e., authoritative] and frightful force.

360. Despite the hard struggle between these absolutely opposed realms—i.e., the other-worldly vs. the this-worldly; or Church vs. Empire—they nevertheless are rooted in a single unity and Idea. Thus the spiritual realm degrades its heaven to the earthly here-and-now, and to a common worldliness, both in actuality and in representation. The worldly realm, on the other hand, raises its abstract independence to the level of thought and to the principle of rational being and knowing, i.e., to the rationality of right and law. Thus the antithesis between them withers away to nothing. The present world has stripped off its barbarism and unjust arbitrariness, and truth has put aside its world of beyond and its casual power. Thus the genuine reconciliation has become objective fact, revealing the *State* to be the image and the actuality of Reason. The State is where self-consciousness finds the actuality of its substantive knowing and willing, as an organic development; in *religion*, similarly, self-consciousness finds the feeling and image of its own truth as an ideal essence; but in *philosophy* it finds the freely grasped cognition of this truth to be one and the same in its complementary manifestations—in the *state*, in *nature* and in the *ideal world*.

This book was set in
ITC Galliard
by
Alexander Typesetting